MASTERS OF WORLD LITERATURE

Published

GEORGE ELIOT by Walter Allen
COLERIDGE by Walter Jackson Bate
T. S. ELIOT by Bernard Bergonzi
GERARD MANLEY HOPKINS by Bernard Bergonzi
MATTHEW ARNOLD by Douglas Bush
JANE AUSTEN by Douglas Bush
JOHN KEATS by Douglas Bush
JOHN MILTON by Douglas Bush
JONATHAN SWIFT by Nigel Dennis
DANTE by Francis Fergusson
STENDHAL by Wallace Fowlie
THOMAS HARDY by Irving Howe
HONORÉ BALZAC by E. J. Oliver
GOLDSMITH by Ricardo Quintana
TENNYSON by Christopher Ricks
THE BRONTËS by Tom Winnifrith

In Preparation

PROUST by William Barrett
FLAUBERT by Jacques Barzun
SAMUEL JOHNSON by James L. Clifford
IBSEN by Harold Clurman
EUGENE O'NEILL by Harold Clurman
EMILY DICKINSON by J. V. Cunningham
YEATS by Douglas N. Archibald
JOYCE by Leon Edel
CONRAD by Elizabeth Hardwick
EMERSON by Alfred Kazin
SHAKESPEARE by Frank Kermode
POE by Dwight Macdonald
CHEKHOV by Howard Moss
FIELDING by Midge Podhoretz
HENRY JAMES by Richard Poirier
MELVILLE by Harold Rosenberg

Gerard Manley Hopkins

MASTERS OF WORLD LITERATURE SERIES

LOUIS KRONENBERGER, GENERAL EDITOR

Gerard Manley Hopkins

by Bernard Bergonzi

MACMILLAN PUBLISHING CO., INC.

NEW YORK

ACKNOWLEDGMENT

The author gratefully acknowledges the permission of The English Province of the Society of Jesus to quote from those writings of Gerard Manley Hopkins, published by the Oxford University Press, that remain in copyright.

Macmillan Publishing Co., Inc.
866 Third Avenue, New York, N.Y. 10022
Collier Macmillan Canada, Ltd.

Library of Congress Cataloging in Publication Data

Bergonzi, Bernard
    Gerard Manley Hopkins.

    (Masters of world literature series)
    Bibliography: p.
    Includes index.
        1. Hopkins, Gerard Manley, 1844–1889.
2. Poets, English—19th century—Biography.
PR4803.H44Z584   1977   821'.8 [B]   76–46337
ISBN 0–02–509950–7

First Printing 1977

Printed in the United States of America

For Gabriel

Each be other's comfort kind

G. M. H.

Contents

Preface

GERARD MANLEY HOPKINS lived a life of remarkable obscurity. To be a Jesuit priest in Victorian England was inevitably to be removed from the mainstream of national life and culture. Even in the Society of Jesus, a small but vigorous and expanding body, Father Hopkins did not achieve distinction; though always a dedicated priest, he encountered such difficulties as pastor and teacher that his superiors could not make effective use of his outstanding intellectual qualities, which had been so finely trained at Oxford. In his lifetime only a few friends knew that he wrote poems, and it was not until nearly thirty years after his death that a collection of them was published. Now, a century after Hopkins began to write the poems of his maturity, he is read and studied throughout the English-speaking world. Hopkins's poems are often difficult, and an explicatory criticism that welcomes, even needs, difficulty has given them its most serious attention. As a result, there are many books, and many more notes and articles, devoted to the interpretation of Hopkins's poetry. Much less has been written about his life, though one has heard of biographies in preparation. Hopkins's first biographer was Father G. F. Lahey, S.J., whose short book appeared in 1930 at a time when Hopkins was beginning to be read and discussed—indeed to be positively imitated by some young English poets—and there was growing public interest in this strange, lately discovered poet. Father Lahey's work deserves respect as a pioneer effort, and as it was written after consulting elderly Jesuits who had known Hopkins forty years before, some of its testimony is of permanent value. But Father Lahey was writing in the Victorian biographical manner, which sought to suppress rather than examine the divisions and struggles within a subject's nature; it is, furthermore, marked by the hint of hagiography that occurs in so many subsequent studies of Hopkins by Jesuit writers. In 1944 Eleanor Ruggles published another biography of Hopkins, a colourful work which, although it draws on the first editions of his journals and correspondence, reads like a novel and does not hesitate to fill gaps in the record with vigorous speculation and invention.

In the present work I have used the flexible formula of the "critical biography" in order to give a more up-to-date account of Hopkins's life and his literary and intellectual development. A reader who is well acquainted with the later editions of Hopkins's letters and journals, together with his sermons and spiritual writings, will find little that is new in what I have written. But those books, though very well edited—particularly the superb second edition of *The Journals and Papers* that appeared in 1959—are not easy for the general reader to use, as they contain so much over-lapping material. In order to render Hopkins's life as a coherent narrative I have drawn heavily but selectively on the rich material they contain. My debt to these books, and their editors—C. C. Abbott, Christopher Devlin, Humphry House and Graham Storey—will be apparent throughout my own study. To these names I will add that of Father Alfred Thomas, S.J., whose *Hopkins the Jesuit* is an informative study of Hopkins's years of training in the

Jesuit order. I am indebted, too, to the *Hopkins Research Bulletin*, which the Hopkins Society has published since 1970. Hopkins's life, though obscure, was not at all uninteresting; it was even, in a quiet way, dramatic. I have tried to place Hopkins within the various contexts in which he lived and worked—Victorian England, Oxford, the Catholic Church, the Jesuit order—though it will be apparent that he was far too original, even eccentric, to fit smoothly into any of these contexts. The passionate originality which impressed and sometimes disconcerted Hopkins's friends and contemporaries shines out of every phase of his life. When Hopkins first became widely read, it was assumed that he was a modern poet born before his time, rebelling against Victorian literary ideals and values; more recently, as a deliberate reaction against this view, it has been argued that Hopkins was really just another Victorian poet, having far more in common with his contemporaries than was at first realized. Both views seem to me equally false, or, for that matter, equally true. In his art as in his life Hopkins was too "counter, original, spare, strange" to fit in anywhere with complete conviction.

For most of this book I discuss Hopkins's poems as they reflect the experiences of his life; my emphasis here is more descriptive than critical. But in the final chapter I try to present a wider critical interpretation and assessment of his mature poetry, together with some discussion of his poetics.

Finally, there are thanks to be recorded. To my wife, for reading the manuscript, and many other things; to the University of Warwick, for sabbatical leave in which to work on this book, and the unfailing helpfulness of its library staff; and to Father Alfred Thomas and the Hopkins Society, for permission to make use of material first published in *Hopkins the Englishman*, which I delivered as the Sixth Annual Lecture of the Society in 1975.

List of Abbreviations Used in Text

The following abbreviations are used to identify quotations from Hopkins's prose writings:

LB.   *The Letters of Gerard Manley Hopkins to Robert Bridges.*
        Edited by C. C. Abbott (London, 1955).

LD.   *The Correspondence of Gerard Manley Hopkins and Richard Watson Dixon.*
        Edited by C. C. Abbott (London, 1955).

FL.   *Further Letters of Gerard Manley Hopkins.*
        Edited by C. C. Abbott. Second Edition (London, 1956).

J.   *The Journals and Papers of Gerard Manley Hopkins.*
        Edited by Humphry House. Completed by Graham Storey. Second Edition (London, 1959).

SD.   *The Sermons and Devotional Writings of Gerard Manley Hopkins.*
        Edited by Christopher Devlin (London, 1959).

Quotations from Hopkins's poetry are from *The Poems.* Edited by W. H. Gardner and N. H. MacKenzie. Fourth Edition (London, 1967).

Gerard Manley Hopkins

1

Schooldays and Oxford

THE HOPKINS FAMILY was comfortably off, cultivated and versatile. Gerard's father, Manley Hopkins, ran a successful marine insurance business in the City of London, and in 1867 published *A Manual of Marine Insurance*. He was also Consul-General in London for the independent Kingdom of Hawaii, a post he had obtained through the good offices of his expatriate younger brother, Charles Hopkins, for many years a prominent member of the Hawaiian government service. Despite the claims of business, Manley extended himself in many directions as a man of letters. He wrote a history of Hawaii. He also published some collections of verse, which showed sensibility without much originality or capacity for development; reviewed poetry for *The Times;* and wrote a novel which remained unpublished. In later years Manley Hopkins developed his professional concern with mathematics, and in 1887 published *The Cardinal Numbers*, with a brief, fanciful contribution from his son Gerard. He was a conventionally religious man, a moderate High Anglican and a Sunday-school teacher. There was, no doubt, an element of the dilettante in Manley Hopkins, and Gerard, though a man of more robust intellectual and creative powers, inherited his father's restless versatility. But Manley must, on the whole, have been an encouraging model. It can only be an advantage for a poet to grow up in a family where the writing of poetry and literary pursuits in general are regarded as a normal part of life. Gerard's mother, Kate Hopkins, though not herself a writer, was a woman of well-developed musical and literary tastes, who read German at a time when it was not common in England, and who took, in later years, a keen interest in her son's poetry. Another benign family influence was Manley's unmarried sister, known as Aunt Annie, an accomplished painter and musician and an amateur student of archaeology. Her water-colour painting of the fifteen-year-old Gerard, now in the National Portrait Gallery in London, is one of the few surviving likenesses of the poet.

Gerard, the Hopkinses' first child, was born at Stratford in Essex on 28th July 1844, the eldest of three sisters and five brothers, several of whom distinguished themselves in art or scholarship. Arthur and Everard both became well known as commercial artists and illustrators and contributors to *Punch;* Arthur also exhibited on occasion at the Royal Academy. Grace was reckoned to be an exceptionally talented musician and amateur composer.

Lionel Hopkins, who died in 1952 at the age of ninety-seven, served as a Consul in China, retired early and became a leading authority on the Chinese language. He did not, however, share the family's artistic inclinations, for his interest in Chinese was entirely linguistic and not at all literary. Indeed, he could not understand why people wrote poetry; "It is the poorest way of putting things," he was once reported as saying. Gerard was not the only member of the family to enter the religious life, for his eldest sister, Milicent, became an Anglican nun. The Hopkins family exemplified the most attractive qualities of Victorian middle-class culture, and provided an admirable environment for a boy who was to be not only a poet and a priest but also, in a less committed way, an artist and musician and student of languages. Only in becoming first a Catholic and then a Jesuit did Gerard depart from his family's values and expectations.

In 1852 the family moved to Oak Hill, Hampstead, then at the edge of open country to the north of London, and lived there for the next thirty-four years. From 1854 Gerard attended Highgate School, a few miles away, as a boarder. The school has had many literary associations, both before and after Hopkins's time there; early in the twentieth century the present Poet Laureate of England, Sir John Betjeman, was a pupil, and T. S. Eliot was briefly a master. Gerard was remembered by his school-fellows as slight of stature and of a mild, likeable, good-humoured temperament, though capable of showing an iron will and great stubbornness when thwarted. One account describes him as a dreamy boy but a fearless climber of trees, which seems an appropriate combination: the branches of the tree provide a delightful and secluded retreat, but can only be attained with some difficulty and even danger. The general impression is of a clever, somewhat precocious boy with an exceptionally refined sensibility, who was, at the same time, sociable and generally popular. Among his school friends were Ernest Coleridge, grandson of the poet, and in later years editor of Coleridge's notebooks, and Marcus Clarke, who went to Australia and made a name as a writer (his novel, *For the Term of His Natural Life*, is still read). Gerard, who was nick-named "Skin," played games with sufficient zeal to command respect but without being an enthusiastic sportsman. Though not extravagantly pious, he read a portion of the New Testament every night because he had promised his mother to do so; despite mild ridicule from the other, less devout occupants of the bedroom, he persisted in his reading and in the end was left undisturbed.

There is more evidence of Gerard's firmness of will and his early tendency towards asceticism. At some point in his teens he decided to abstain from all liquids for a week (or even, incredibly, in another version for three weeks). The ostensible reason was simply to win a bet, though there was a deeper intention of sharing the sufferings of seamen and testing human

powers of endurance. Gerard won the bet, though with a
blackened tongue and other signs of physical distress. He was
then punished for the whole rash undertaking by the heavy-
handed headmaster of Highgate School, Dr. John Bradley Dyne,
with whom Gerard was on the worst possible terms. In May
1862 they had a memorably fierce encounter when Gerard
stubbornly defended himself in the face of some crass act of
injustice inflicted by Dyne: "I was driven out of patience and
cheeked him wildly, and he blazed into me with his riding-
whip" (FL 2).

Yet whatever vendetta Dyne conducted against the boy he
could not escape the fact that Gerard was an academic high-
flyer who easily mastered the predominantly classical curricu-
lum of the English grammar-school of that time. A collection
of handsomely bound prize-books remains as evidence of his
progress, and so does the gold medal awarded as the school
prize for Latin verse in 1862. A few months after the riding-
whip incident, Dyne had to sign, with whatever reluctance, the
bookplates in yet one more award, a three-volume edition of
Motley's *Rise of the Dutch Republic*. This may well have been
Gerard's last prize, as the following year he left Highgate for
Oxford. Up to the very point of his departure he was harried
by Dyne, whom he contemptuously referred to as the "Patriarch
of the Old Dispensation": in March 1863 he was complaining
that Dyne had made him sit a quite unnecessary examination
before leaving the school. Dyne's side of the contention will
never be known; though a harsh disciplinarian, he was in some
respects a very successful headmaster, who built up Highgate
School considerably during his years there, and he was ac-
counted a good teacher of classics. But he seems to have found
Gerard Hopkins intolerably provocative, despite—indeed, perhaps because of—his intellectual brilliance. Gerard, for his
part, was glad to see the back of him, and of Highgate School.
Years later he told his correspondent Canon Dixon: "the truth
is I had no love for my schooldays and wished to banish the
rememberance of them." Hopkins first encountered Dixon at
Highgate, though the two barely knew each other there. In

1861 Dixon, then a young clergyman, spent a few months as a junior master at the school. Hopkins remembered him quite well, and in 1878 wrote to express his admiration for Dixon's poetry, thereby beginning the long and fruitful correspondence between the two poets. He was gratified to find that Dixon, despite his short stay at the school, preserved a clear recollection of "a pale young boy, very light and active, with a very meditative and intellectual face, whose name, if I am not vastly mistaken, was yours." Hopkins, he seemed to remember, had also won a prize for an English poem.

This poem was "The Escorial," which won the school prize in 1860. Dated Easter of that year, it is an extraordinarily assured composition for a boy not yet sixteen, and there is a sardonic sense of occasion in the epigraph, a line of Greek from Theocritus which means "and I compete, like a frog against the cicadas." The poem describes in fourteen Spenserian stanzas the celebrated Spanish royal palace, built on the ground-plan of a grid-iron to commemorate the martyrdom of St. Lawrence. The subject was, no doubt, provided by the school authorities, but Hopkins found it congenial since it enabled him to express what were already engrossing interests, and which were to remain so throughout his adult life: ascetic religion, architecture, painting. The difficult stanza form is handled with great skill, with echoes of Spenser in occasional words or phrases. Spenser may well have been mediated to Hopkins by Keats, and it is certainly Keats who provided the dominant influence on the poem, particularly the would-be medieval Keats of "The Eve of St. Agnes." "The Escorial" draws heavily on that poem, in its basic cadences as well as in its diction and imagery. Yet there are suggestions, too, of the lyrical melancholy of the early Tennyson:

> Then through the afternoon the summer beam
> Slop'd on the galleries; upon the wall
> Rich Titians faded; in the straying gleam
> The motes in ceaseless eddy shine and fall
> Into the cooling gloom; till slowly all
> Dimm'd in the long accumulated dust. . . .

"The Escorial" is, undoubtedly, a highly imitative poem; but such intelligent imitation is the best way, perhaps the only possible way, for a very young poet to acquire a style of his own. Hopkins may already have acquired fluency in writing verse from Dyne's method of teaching classics, which involved translating Latin verse into English, as well as the more usual practice of translating English verse into Latin.

In addition to its stylistic accomplishment "The Escorial" is full of historical and artistic references, of which Robert Bridges remarked: "the history seems competent and the artistic knowledge precocious." Particularly precocious were the marginal notes with which Hopkins adorned each stanza, pointing up the references in a showy though pardonable display of youthful erudition. The amount that the fifteen-year-old boy knew is indeed striking, and is, in part, a tribute to the high level of formal education that he received at Highgate School. But it also indicates the atmosphere of unemphatic learning and artistic achievement that pervaded the Hopkins household; significantly, the only surviving manuscript of "The Escorial" was transcribed by Manley Hopkins. In the sixth stanza Hopkins, preparing to describe the architecture of the palace, engages in the familiar Miltonic device of the extended negative comparison to make some informed reflections on Gothic architecture:

> No finish'd proof was this of Gothic grace
> With flowing tracery engemming rays
> Of colour in high casements face to face;
> And foliag'd crownals (pointing how the ways
> Of art best follow nature). . . .

These lines look forward to Hopkins's later interest in Gothic, particularly in the work of contemporary neo-Gothic architects like William Butterfield. Hopkins's interest in the subject was focussed and strengthened by his subsequent reading of Ruskin; indeed, he may well have read some Ruskin as early as 1860. But his remarks on Gothic in "The Escorial" might also have owed something to J. H. Parker's *Introduction to the*

Study of Gothic Architecture, which he received as a Christmas present when he was thirteen.

A few other poems survive from Hopkins's schooldays. "A Vision of the Mermaids," from Christmas 1862, is a narrative poem of some hundred and fifty lines, written in couplets and decidedly Keatsian in its movement and its densely grouped, sensuous images that attempt to load every rift with ore. The manuscript of the poem reflects Hopkins's aspirations as pictorial artist as well as poet, for it is ornamented with an elaborate though rather wooden pen-and-ink drawing of mermaids contemplating the setting sun. At about the same time Hopkins wrote "Winter with the Gulf Stream," which was much shorter and in some ways more interesting. It was published in *Once a Week* in February 1863, and was one of the very few poems by Hopkins to be printed in his lifetime. It is a piece of natural description in terza rima; the use of this form, which Hopkins handled adroitly, is an early sign of his capacity for stylistic innovation and development. Hopkins thought well enough of this poem to revise it extensively in later years, and it is the revised version, certainly an improvement on the original, which is included in the *Collected Poems.* Hopkins's revisions tended to make the diction sharper and more individual, as is apparent if we compare the successive versions of the poem's closing lines. The original conclusion reads:

> All ways the molten colours run:
> Till, sinking ever more and more
>
> Into an azure mist, the sun
> Drops down engulf'd, his journey done.

The revision reads:

> The waxen colours weep and run,
> And slendering to his burning rim
>
> Into the flat blue mist the sun
> Drops out and all our day is done.

Hopkins went up to Balliol College, Oxford, in April 1863. He was, not surprisingly, much happier at university than at school, and throughout his life remembered Oxford with particular affection as the "Towery city and branchy between towers" of his sonnet "Duns Scotus's Oxford." Matthew Arnold, at that time Professor of Poetry, acknowledged and tried to resist the peculiar, insidious charm of Oxford, "whispering from her towers the last enchantments of the Middle Age. . . . Home of lost causes and forsaken beliefs." It was still the cluster of ancient buildings, colleges, churches and libraries pictured by Rudolf Ackermann in his prints of the early 1800s, with the open country coming almost up to the grey stone walls. In the 1860s Oxford was the University and the University was Oxford. It would be many decades before Oxford grew into a large manufacturing city and a stronghold of the motor industry. In the first half of the nineteenth century Oxford was indeed beautiful and placid; but the university was also lax and complacently torpid, a finishing school for young English gentlemen rather than a place of committed teaching and intellectual enquiry. Reforms came eventually, imposed by the government on a reluctant university in the 1850s. Already, in the twenties and thirties, some individual colleges had reformed themselves and raised their intellectual standards, thanks to the efforts of enlightened and energetic college heads. Oriel, where John Henry Newman had once been a junior fellow, was one, and Balliol was another. In 1863 the Master of Balliol was Robert Scott, a rather remote man of less emphatic personality than his reforming predecessor, Dr. Jennings, though still remembered as one of the compilers of the famous Greek lexicon, Liddell and Scott. Balliol was already a college of the highest scholastic standards and expectations, and this reputation was to be further enhanced when Benjamin Jowett became Master in 1870. Jowett was University Professor of Greek and a dedicated, immensely hard-working college tutor. He was a controversial figure as a leader of the Broad Church faction in the all-pervasive ecclesiastical politics of the day. In Balliol itself he was a formidable force; still hurt at having been beaten by Scott in the election for the mastership in 1854, Jowett gained increasing control of college policy through the votes of his supporters among the fellows. He was

one of Hopkins's tutors, and at their first interview in April
1863 he told the young man to take great pains with his weekly
essay—"as on it would depend my success more than on anything else, (which by the way was not a Highgatian theory)"—
and not to have any debts beyond the end of term. "When you
can get him to talk," Hopkins reported to his mother, "he is
amusing, but when the opposite it is terribly embarrassing."
Jowett's long, embarrassed silences and lack of conventional
small talk were notorious.

Yet however illustrious their tutors, the undergraduates did,
in a sense, educate each other, as Newman acknowledged in
The Idea of a University. In a college like Balliol the presence
of so many bright and aspiring young men, who often sys-
tematically studied together, was at the heart of the educational
process. A vivid if idealized impression of what Balliol was like
in the sixties was left by a college contemporary of Hopkins's,
Martin Geldart, in his autobiographical novel, *A Son of Belial*
(1882):

> Never in all my life before or since was I among a company
> of men so young and ardent, yet so utterly devoted to plain
> living and high thinking. Never was I in an intellectual
> atmosphere so fearless and so free. . . . It was a new experi-
> ence to me altogether—to me who had been brought up to
> regard Ritualism and Rationalism as the two right arms of
> the devil, to find myself suddenly launched among a lot of
> men who were some of them Ritualists of the deepest dye,
> some of them Rationalists, some of them Positivists, some of
> them Materialists, all eager in advancing their respective
> views, and yet all ready to listen with courtesy to their
> respective opponents.

Geldart's description of the undergraduate community in
terms of religious divisions is significant. In the sixties the
University of Oxford was not only a closed religious corpora-
tion, but an exclusively Anglican one. All members of the
university, from undergraduates to professors, had to adhere
to the Thirty Nine Articles, the foundation of Anglican doctrine. Of course the profession of faith was sometimes nominal

or even hypocritical, as it presumably was for those young men described by Geldart as rationalists or materialists. But the interpretation of the Thirty Nine Articles was flexible. Attendance at chapel was compulsory, and all fellows of colleges, whatever subjects they taught, had to be clergymen and celibate. This last requirement was, however, breaking down in the sixties and two of Hopkins's tutors were among the first holders of non-clerical fellowships: Walter Pater at Brasenose, and T. H. Green at Balliol.

University religion provided much more than an opportunity for private or public devotion. It could offer political excitement in the clashes and intrigues between different ecclesiastical factions; there was satisfaction for the intellect in the continual arguments about questions of theological interpretation or scriptural exegesis; and outstanding preachers combined edification with the pleasures of performance, as Newman had done in his Anglican days from the pulpit of St. Mary's. If unbelief was a growing threat to institutionalized Christianity in Victorian England as a whole, its presence was less immediately felt at Oxford, if only because the university was, by statute, exclusively Anglican. Even so, Walter Pater, as a young don, aroused hostility by his unguarded expression of anti-Christian sentiments, until he learnt to preserve a prudent silence. The major collisions and polemics at Oxford were between the three principal camps within the Anglican establishment. The High Church party, otherwise Anglo-Catholic or Tractarian, had been prominent since the Oxford Movement of the 1830s, when the publication of *Tracts for the Times,* affirming the importance of ecclesiastical traditions and disciplines and the value of ancient forms of devotion, had aroused a new kind of religious fervour. The Tractarian case was that the Church of England was truly Catholic, preserving the Apostolic succession in a middle way between the opposed errors of Roman Catholicism and Protestantism. The original Oxford Movement had barely survived the defection for Rome of J. H. Newman in 1845, followed by many of his disciples. But in the Oxford of the 1860s the High Church faction was conspicuous and powerful, under the leadership of E. B. Pusey, Professor of

Hebrew and one of the original Tractarians. Pusey, a harsh but magnetic personality, embittered by the early death of his much-loved wife and the departure to Rome of so many of his former colleagues and able young disciples, was supported by his principal lieutenant and subsequent biographer, Canon H. P. Liddon of Christ Church. Against the High Church camp was set the Low Church or Evangelicals, who proudly proclaimed their four-square Protestantism and strict adherence to scripture. Both Tractarians and Evangelicals were opposed to the Broad Church party, of which Jowett was a distinguished leader. The Broad Church played down dogma and the supernatural and tried to reconcile Christianity with the development of modern thought, or what the original Tractarians had witheringly denounced as the "march of mind." In 1860 *Essays and Reviews*, a collection of papers by Jowett and other Broad Church thinkers, aroused a storm of scandalized protest; unsuccessful attempts were made to have the book suppressed by the action of the ecclesiastical courts and even to have Jowett himself tried for heresy. It was felt that the Broad Church movement was a Trojan horse that would betray organized Christianity to contemporary infidelity; certainly it was not always easy to see a distinction between the Broad Church version of non-dogmatic, ethically responsive Christianity and the devout, even reverent agnosticism which, rather than dogmatic atheism, was the characteristic mode of non-belief among eminent Victorians. In the face of the Broad Church threat there was a tendency for Tractarians and Evangelicals to sink their differences.

Hopkins, no doubt because of his High Church family background and his strong aesthetic tendencies, was readily drawn to the Puseyite camp. He had not been in Oxford more than a few weeks when he started attending one of the attractions of High Church Oxford: Canon Liddon's Sunday evening lectures, which were followed by tea, coffee and conversation. In time Hopkins induced Martin Geldart to accompany him to these occasions, though Geldart's own family background was Evangelical and he was to become finally a Unitarian. Geldart has left a sharp account of Liddon as a gaunt, cadaverous figure with a sweet, somewhat sickly smile, especially when being sarcastic at the expense of rationalists and other adversaries: "He was a popular University preacher, an exceedingly voluble rhetorician, crouching in his pulpit in a cat-like attitude as though ready to spring on his adversary, which he did with feline ferocity as opportunity occurred." Liddon became Hopkins's regular confessor, and when Hopkins became a Roman Catholic in 1866 Liddon made great efforts to get him to reconsider or at least delay his decision. Compared with the rigid Pusey, Liddon, a much younger man, had a flexible and sensitive temperament. For the time being, though, Gerard Hopkins was secure in his adherence to the Anglican Church. Compared to the original Tractarians of the 1830s, the Anglo-Catholics of the 1860s were given to ritualistic devotions, which greatly appealed to the young poet. Geldart described Hopkins as "my Ritualistic friend." But Hopkins, though inclined to be intellectually intolerant, was never so in his personal relations, and always acknowledged worth wherever he found it. Geldart records that Hopkins admired the "purity" of such a pillar of the Broad Church as Jowett: "what had he been but a Catholic he would have called his 'saintliness'—as something which struck him more in Professor Jewell [Jowett] than in almost any other."

Though religion was a major preoccupation of Hopkins's life at Oxford, there were many others. The diaries that he kept from 1863 to 1866 show the remarkable variety of his interests. They do, of course, contain ordinary diary material: notes on social encounters and the addresses of friends and tradesmen, together with occasional jottings about life or art. But there are also precise Ruskinian descriptions of natural or architectural objects, sometimes accompanied by equally Ruskinian drawings. There are lists of books read or to be read, of pictures or buildings looked at, critically or appreciatively. There is early evidence of one of Hopkins's central and abiding interests in lists of words and speculations about their possible derivations and cross-relations. This kind of linguistic enquiry was called for by the course in Honour Moderations for which Hopkins was reading, but, as with other under-graduate exercises, he made it express his literary inclinations. Alan Ward, in the "Philological Notes" forming Appendix III of the *Journals and Papers*, has paid tribute to the accuracy of many of Hopkins's linguistic guesses and speculations, re-marking: "What a philologist he might have made!" Mr. Ward has shown how the philological and the poetic were related in Hopkins's scheme of things:

> Many of the lists could be considered as verbal exercises, sense-variations on a formal scheme; some even as miniature poetic compositions in which the meaning or idea common to the individual words forms the subject of the composition, which is given shape by the similarity in form of each word to the other.

Thus, when Hopkins writes: "Grind, gride, gird, grit, groat, grate, great . . .," we already have a faint anticipation of the method of his late poems where "thoughts against thoughts in groans grind." Hopkins's philological investigations dwell not only on Teutonic, Latin and Greek words, but extend even to African words taken from Speke's *Journal of the Discovery of the Nile*.

The diaries contain drafts of Hopkins's early poems and a few notes on his state of mind and religious ideas, though it seems that the full account of his spiritual development was kept in a separate diary, now lost. The undergraduate diaries make very apparent Hopkins's relentless intellectual curiosity, a quality which led him, throughout his career, to dissipate rather than concentrate his interests (though it is something to have so many interests to dissipate). This breadth of curiosity did not, however, deflect Hopkins from the seemingly effortless mastery of academic work. Like most of his contemporaries he was reading for the B.A. in Classics, known at Oxford as Literae Humaniores, which comprised the study of Greek and Latin language and literature, philosophy and ancient history. It was a four-year course, with a major examination, Honour Moderations or "Mods," after two years, and another, known as "Greats," at the end of the course. Despite the many distractions, Hopkins satisfied general expectations by obtaining a first-class pass in both parts.

The personal qualities which had brought Hopkins popularity at Highgate gained him many new friends at Oxford, and years later those who had known him as an undergraduate still recalled his marked but unaffected charm. Long walks were a favourite way of combining exercise with ardent conversation, and soon after arriving at Oxford Hopkins discovered the pleasures of the river: "a canoe in the Cherwell must be the summit of human happiness," he told his mother. There were breakfasts to attend, too. These elaborate social occasions, with several courses of fish, eggs and meat, were a prominent feature of Oxford life at that time (and indeed lingered on until fairly recently). So were small wine-parties in undergraduates' or tutors' rooms after dinner in the evenings. Needless to say, it was an exclusively male world. The upper-class and upper-middle-class culture of Victorian England was dominated by the principle of "male bonding"; from preparatory school to public school to university a boy was brought up in the exclusive company of his own sex at both work and play. Only those who were unusually determined, or had the right kind of family, had much opportunity to meet girls. Many Victorian gentlemen married late in life, or not at all, and the "confirmed bachelor," seldom heard of now unless as a recognised homosexual, was a familiar figure. As a result of this male exclusiveness the friendships of young men were sometimes very emotional, with avowed expressions of affection and hints of jealousy or dissatisfaction at some word or incident. This can be disconcerting to the modern reader, who may misunderstand the prevailing conventions and misinterpret the feelings involved. Nor was it only young men who expressed themselves in effusive ways; Benjamin Disraeli, as a middle-aged and happily married politician, could write to his friend Lord Henry Lennox: "I can only tell you that I love you." That homosexuality existed, was even to some extent fostered, in the public schools and universities need not be doubted. But not all emotional friendships between young men were homosexual. The point needs to be made so that Hopkins's Oxford friendships, which did tend to a certain intensity of sentiment, can be seen in context.

Hopkins lost touch with many of his Oxford friends when he became a Jesuit in 1868, though correspondence would sometimes be resumed after a long lapse. One of those he continued to hear from was Alexander Wood, a Scot of Presbyterian upbringing, who was Hopkins's contemporary, not at Balliol but at the adjacent and rival college of Trinity. Hopkins and Wood made a similar spiritual progress and were received into the Roman Catholic Church at about the same time in 1866. As undergraduates they were close friends, who enjoyed canoeing together whilst reciting aloud long passages from Scott's "Marmion." On one occasion Hopkins took Wood into the nearby country to show him, as a curiosity, a farmer's waggon made entirely of wood. Hopkins, who was noted for a whimsical sense of humour and a thoroughly Victorian taste for puns and word-play, apparently enjoyed the juxtaposition of Wood and wood. (An anticipation of James Joyce's proud possession of a view of Cork framed in cork.)

Another lasting friendship was with Alexander Baillie, also a Scot, and a Balliol contemporary. Some of Hopkins's most engaging correspondence is to be found in his letters to Baillie, written during university vacations. These letters, reminiscent of Keats's, are charming and high-spirited, full of lively personal responses to books and paintings and ideas, and infused with Hopkins's characteristic love of argument. In one of these letters, dated 10th September 1864, Hopkins sets down at length his theories about the language of poetry; it is an important source for his early critical opinions. After leaving Oxford, Baillie entered the law, visited North Africa and became something of an authority on Egyptian history and culture. In his later letters to Baillie Hopkins engages in painfully abstruse discussions of fine points of Egyptology, a topic which was one of the less profitable preoccupations of his later years. Baillie always remembered him with great affection, and told Mrs. Hopkins after his friend's death: "He is the one figure which fills my whole memory of my Oxford life. There is hardly a reminiscence with which he is not associated. All my intellectual growth, and a very large proportion of the happiness of those Oxford days, I owe to his companionship" (FL 449).

But of all the friendships that Hopkins made at Oxford, the most enduring and important was with Robert Bridges. Born in the same year as Hopkins, Bridges was an old Etonian from a long-established family with minor aristocratic connections. He was an undergraduate at Corpus Christi College and, like Hopkins, a devout Anglo-Catholic. He was a member of Pusey's Brotherhood of the Holy Trinity, a prestigious body to which Hopkins was also elected but in the end declined to join because of some personal scruple. Later their spiritual paths diverged sharply, for Bridges gave up Christianity altogether, though their friendship was unaffected. Bridges was a prolific but reticent poet, in a cool, neo-classical, Parnassian manner which was very unlike Hopkins's idiosyncratic poetic idiom. But Bridges and Hopkins had a shared interest in prosodic and metrical experiment, a not uncommon product of classical training. After leaving Oxford, Bridges became a doctor and served for many years in busy London hospitals. But in early middle age he abandoned his medical career to devote himself exclusively to literature. Though never regarded as more than a very able minor poet, he attracted a certain admiring audience and in 1913 was appointed Poet Laureate, a post he held until his death in 1930. He is of crucial importance in the story of Hopkins as man and poet. When Hopkins began writing poetry again in 1875, after several years of silence, he sent Bridges the manuscripts of all his poems and Bridges carefully kept or transcribed them. Hopkins's letters to Bridges form a substantial volume, and are full of revelations, not only of Hopkins's ideas about life and art, but also of the day-to-day workings of a remarkable intelligence that was both subtle and, at times, startlingly tough and assertive. It is true that Bridges's regard for Hopkins was tinged with patronage, and that he had an inadequate understanding of Hopkins's aims and achievements as a poet. Nevertheless, it is to Bridges that we owe the fact of Hopkins's survival as a poet. After an initial rebuff from the Jesuit magazine, *The Month*, in 1876, Hopkins lost interest in trying to publish his poems, indeed became positively hostile to the idea in his painfully scrupulous fashion, and was happy to leave their fate to posterity. Bridges ensured that the poems were preserved, and after a long delay, which he judged to be necessary, arranged for their publication. In doing so Bridges served not only the memory of a long dead friend, but English poetry itself, in a way that must be acknowledged, despite his somewhat imperceptive preface to the *Poems* of 1918 and his occasional misguided tampering with Hopkins's texts.

It is likely that Hopkins was much more influenced at Oxford by his friends than by his tutors. Nevertheless, Jowett must have made a lasting impression, as he did on all the young men he taught. Other Balliol tutors were less significant figures, though Hopkins liked and admired the Reverend James Riddell, who was said to be an outstandingly good teacher of classics. But Riddell died suddenly of a heart attack in 1866, much to Hopkins's distress. Another Balliol tutor, the Reverend Edward Woolcombe, was a kindly, ineffectual Tractarian who regarded himself as a pillar of the college. One of Hopkins's contemporaries remarked of Woolcombe that "what he gave us was all the small change of scholarship, most conscientiously doled out. But the one thing missing was grasp." A man of much greater calibre was Thomas Hill Green, who tutored Hopkins in philosophy. Green, a moderate Hegelian and author of *Prolegomena to Ethics,* is still an important name in the history of nineteenth-century British philosophy. We do not know much about their tutorial relationship, though one of Hopkins's surviving undergraduate essays, on "The Position of Plato in the Greek World," was initialled by Green. Early in his Balliol career, probably before he knew him, Hopkins had superciliously dismissed Green as "of a rather offensive style of infidelity, and naturally dislikes the beauties of nature." But later he developed a much higher opinion of him, which appears to have been reciprocated. Unlike Jowett, whose aim as a teacher was to develop and draw out his students' own ideas, Green was of a doctrinaire cast of mind and tried to make his pupils follow his own lines of thought. But the young Hopkins, already a formidably independent and argumentative thinker, would certainly have resisted attempts at indoctrination. After Green's premature death in 1882 Hopkins told Baillie: "I always liked and admired poor Green. He seemed to me upright in mind and life."

The most intellectually advanced of Hopkins's tutors was Walter Pater; one would like to know the nature of their discussions and the extent of Pater's influence on Hopkins, but the evidence is scanty. Pater, a young don of twenty-seven, had not long been a fellow of Brasenose when, as Hopkins noted in his journal, they went for a walk together one fine but cold evening in April 1866 (the ancient tradition of peripatetic teaching was still very much alive at Oxford). Despite Hopkins's marked distaste for infidelity and irreligion, he seems to have tolerated Pater's irreverences—at least, he merely records in his journal, without comment, an occasion when Pater talked for two hours against Christianity—and to have developed genuinely friendly feelings towards him. He was disappointed in his hope for an invitation to visit Pater in Devon in the summer of 1867, but they met in London the following year, not long before Hopkins entered the Jesuit order. Ten years later Hopkins was pleased and flattered to hear from Bridges that Pater still remembered and took an interest in him. And in the months during 1878 and 1879 that Hopkins spent as an assistant priest at St. Aloysius, Oxford, Pater was, as he noted, "one of the men I saw most of."

When Hopkins was an undergraduate Pater was just beginning his career as a critic of art and literature, which was to establish him, with *The Renaissance* in 1873, as an important if elusive figure in the Aesthetic Movement. Hopkins himself was a keen if unsystematic speculator on questions of aesthetics, and it is easy to conclude that he was considerably influenced by Pater's developing thoughts about art. Indeed, that conclusion has more than once been confidently drawn. But tangible evidence is lacking, and one can only proceed by guesses and inferences. It is true that both Hopkins and Pater stressed the importance of the individual moment, the sudden insight or illumination, but their frames of reference were very different. Pater's view of life, as he described it in the celebrated "Conclusion" to *The Renaissance,* was directed towards total scepticism about ultimate or systematic beliefs and values; Hopkins was an absolute believer, finding the glory of God in the momentary revelation of beauty. Pater saw existence as flux; Hopkins was constantly struck by the singularity and substantiality of things. It is true that by degrees Pater moved closer, in feeling if not in intellectual conviction, to the kind of wistful, ritualistic Christianity he described in *Marius the Epicurean.* But Hopkins, though an emotional ritualist in his Anglican days, was, as a Roman Catholic and still more as a Jesuit, an exponent of precise, dogmatic theology, defined with scholastic exactness, and showed little interest in ritual or the merely aesthetic aspects of religion.

A likely place to see Pater's influence would be in the longest and most ambitious of Hopkins's undergraduate essays, "On the Origin of Beauty: A Platonic Dialogue." But the essay is dated 12th May 1865, a year before the first reference to Pater as Hopkins's tutor. One may doubt whether Pater, still a very new fellow of Brasenose, had at that time fully developed his aesthetic views, which were not given public expression until his essays on Winckleman and Rossetti appeared in 1867. "On the Origin of Beauty" may have been a paper written for the Hexameron, Canon Liddon's High Church essay society; writing to Baillie in January 1865, Hopkins refers to "toiling through an essay for the Hexameron" on questions of Truth and Beauty. The dialogue is a most attractive piece of writing, convincing in the lightly fictional framework and adroit in the handling of ideas. A conversation about art and the nature of beauty takes place in New College gardens, and the Socratic central speaker is the lately appointed Professor of Aesthetics. There was no such post at Oxford, but there were current discussions about institutionalizing the teaching of art and art history, and in 1870 John Ruskin was appointed to a newly established Chair of Art. In Hopkins's dialogue the Professor is a distinctly Ruskinian figure, expounding the kind of aesthetic

doctrine for which Ruskin was already famous. The Professor's
analysis of the shape of a chestnut-fan, for instance, directly
recalls the discussion of leaves in Volume V of *Modern Painters*.
Ruskin is frequently recalled in Hopkins's early writings and
drawings. In July 1863 he wrote to Baillie: "I am sketching (in
pencil chiefly) a good deal. I venture to hope you will approve
of some of the sketches in a Ruskinese point of view." He
describes his attraction to certain subjects, particularly the ash-
tree: "the present fury is the ash, and perhaps barley and two
shapes of growth in leaves and one in tree boughs and also a
conformation of fine-weather cloud . . ." (FL 202). The drawings
are parallelled by the immensely precise descriptions of nature
that we find in Hopkins's diaries and journals, revealing a
disciplined concentration on the object in front of him that was
clearly derived from Ruskin. It was from Ruskin that Hopkins
learnt to look in such a patient way, not only at leaves and
branches, but also at rocks and water and the shape of clouds.
It is a little puzzling to find *Modern Painters* mentioned in a
list of "books to be read" in Hopkins's diary for early 1865
because by that time he had given every sign of a thorough
acquaintance with Ruskin's celebrated book. But he may have
meant to indicate his intention of rereading *Modern Painters*,
or of reading one particular volume that he had not yet caught
up with; perhaps the fifth, which so influenced "On the Origin
of Beauty," completed later in the same year.

This list of books exemplifies Hopkins's intellectual and
literary curiosity. There are books on architecture, and a life of
Savonarola, the Florentine ascetic and spiritual teacher for
whom the young Hopkins had a marked admiration. There
are also two famous works from opposed Anglican camps,
whose presence is mildly surprising because one would have
thought that Hopkins, so voracious a reader and so interested
in religious controversy, would already have read them. They
are the Anglo-Catholic *Tracts for the Times* and the Broad
Church *Essays and Reviews*, which had provoked incessant
controversy since it had appeared in 1860. The titles of novels
by Dickens, Thackeray and George Eliot reflect another facet
of Hopkins's eclectic literary tastes, for throughout his life he

was a keen reader of contemporary fiction. A significant name on the list is that of Matthew Arnold, for whose criticism Hopkins always showed great respect even whilst detesting his religious opinions.

As an undergraduate Hopkins wrote many poems and drafted many others. It seems to have been his intention to destroy all his early poems before becoming a Jesuit; this, at least, is the most probable interpretation of an enigmatic reference in his journal in the spring of 1868 to the "massacre of the innocents." Nevertheless, enough manuscripts have survived to give one some idea of Hopkins's first phase as a poet. The principal impression one gets, both from the completed poems and from the drafts and fragments, is of stylistic variety. Whereas most young poets write to express themselves directly, Hopkins is more interested in experimenting with as many different ways of writing English verse as he can, so we find sonnets, songs, ballads and unfinished fragments of narrative or dramatic verse. The variety is a little bewildering, reflecting the author's restless energy of mind (throughout his life he was quicker to begin projects than to complete them); but it also points to Hopkins's professionalism as a poet, a quality which finally asserted itself when he entered the second, mature phase of his poetic career in 1875. The themes are mostly religious, with a certain Anglo-Catholic atmosphere. "For a Picture of St. Dorothea," for instance, is about a virgin-martyr of the early Church and reflects the Tractarian taste for hagiography. In "Easter Communion" the young Hopkins seems to be noting with approval the flagellatory practices of some extreme Anglo-Catholics:

> Pure fasted faces draw unto this feast:
> God comes all sweetness to your Lenten lips.
> You striped in secret with breath-taking whips,
> Those crookèd rough-scored chequers may be pieced
> To crosses meant for Jesu's. . . .

One of the best known of the early poems, "Heaven-Haven," is sub-titled "A nun takes the veil." It is an exquisite lyric, though pervaded with Pre-Raphaelite religiosity, somewhat akin in feeling to Charles Allston Collins's painting "Convent Thoughts":

> I have desired to go
> Where springs not fail,
> To fields where flies no sharp and sided hail
> And a few lilies blow.

The last line of that stanza echoes a Keatsian phrase—"And no birds sing"—which recurs like a haunting tune throughout nineteenth-century poetry from Keats himself to the *fin de siècle*. The influence of Keats on Hopkins has already been referred to, and the traces are frequent in his undergraduate poetry, as, for instance, in the strong but rejected sensuousness of "The Habit of Perfection." Yet other English poets were at least as influential. Thus, the title of "Heaven-Haven" suggests a line by George Herbert, "These seas are tears, and Heaven the haven," and certainly Herbert was a major influence in the development of Hopkins as a poet. "New Readings" can best be described as an intelligent pastiche of Herbert:

> Although the letter said
> On thistles that men look not grapes to gather
> I read the story rather
> How soldiers platting thorns around CHRIST'S Head
> Grapes grew and drops of wine were shed.

One of Hopkins's closest friends at Oxford, William Addis, wrote long after his death: "George Herbert was his strongest tie to the English Church," and there are frequent expressions in Hopkins's correspondence of his love of Herbert. The reading of Herbert would have put Hopkins in touch with a more robust and intellectually coherent kind of religious poetry than anything written by his contemporaries. Among other things, Hopkins learnt from Herbert the poetic use of central Christian traditions of iconography and typology. Herbert showed it was possible to use a plain style and diction for spiritual ends; above all, he wrote a poetry that, though humble and devout, was also argumentative and dialectical. The lesson was not lost on Hopkins, whose temperament needed precisely this combination of qualities. Although he seems not to have read the equally argumentative if more dramatic poetry of John Donne, he did admire another master of seventeenth-century religious poetry, Henry Vaughan, of whom he remarked in a letter to Canon Dixon in 1879: "He has more glow and freedom than Herbert but less fragrant sweetness." In the second version of his poem on St. Dorothea Hopkins writes: "It waned into the world of light," which might be an allusion to Vaughan's famous line, "They are all gone into the world of light."

Other voices, too, are audible. Reading through the early poems and drafts, one often comes across passages that seem like deliberate exercises in the manner of other poets. Shakespeare, for instance:

> What then when these lines are dead
> And coldly do belie the thought of thee?
> I'll lay them by, and freshly turn instead
> To thy not-staled uncharted memory.

Mostly it is Hopkins's contemporaries who are imitated; Rossetti or Morris in the literary ballad, "The Queen's Crowning," and Browning in "A Voice from the World":

> I stood; but does she stand or kneel?
> I strove to look; I lost the trick
> Of nerve; the clammy ball was dry.

The dominant presence in this last poem, however, is Christina Rossetti, and it was written as a deliberate reply to her "The Convent Threshold." At this stage Hopkins was still learning his craft, and it was from such eclectic imitations that he was to forge in time his own profoundly original manner. Already, in his undergraduate poems, there are occasional hints of the stylistic characteristics of his mature poetry, as in "The Habit of Perfection":

> This ruck and reel which you remark
> Coils, keeps, and teases simple sight.

If stylistic imitation was one way of learning to be a poet, another was the training of perception in ways taught, above all, by Ruskin. Thus in a diary entry for 1865 Hopkins writes:

Notes for poetry. Feathery rows of young corn. Ruddy, furred and branchy tops of the elms backed by rolling cloud.
Frieze of sculpture, long-membered vines tugged at by reaching pursuant fauns, and lilies [J 57].

The detailed Ruskinian notations of natural phenomena were not always particularly poetic; sometimes they ran to a visual pedantry, an attempt to render in words what really requires the pen or pencil. Yet they could provide Hopkins with the starting-point for a poem, and twentieth-century readers, familiar with the Imagist tradition, may be more ready than Hopkins's contemporaries to see the essence of a poem in such fragments as:

> Now more precisely touched in light and gloom,
> The place in the east with earliest milky morn
> Rounds its still-purpling centre-darks of cloud.

Or:

> The stars were packed so close that night
> They seemed to press and stare
> And gather in like hurdles bright
> The liberties of air.

Or:

> The time was late and the wet yellow woods
> Told off their leaves along the piercing gale.

Inevitably our reading of Hopkins's early poetry is affected by our knowledge of his later work. Looked at in isolation, his undergraduate poems show remarkable skill, interesting formal variety and an occasional memorable perception, though their mostly religious themes are conventional enough. The two best are, perhaps, the two best-known, often anthologised since Bridges included them in the 1918 *Poems:* "Heaven-Haven" and "The Habit of Perfection." But the gap between even the best of the early poems and "The Wreck of the *Deutschland*" and what followed it is immense. Hindsight, certainly, enables us to see hints and implications that were to be picked up in the mature work; and, as I have remarked, the young Hopkins was strikingly professional in his range of technical accomplishment. Yet if the early poems were all that survived of Hopkins's work, they would scarcely be read and remembered today. Even as an undergraduate Hopkins was never single-minded as a poet; the Romantic or Symbolist notion of poetry as a cause requiring a sense of religious dedication in the poet—as when Joyce's Stephen Dedalus renounced Catholicism for the religion of art—would have struck Hopkins as either unintelligible or blasphemous. Temperamentally, too, his inclination was to dissipate rather than concentrate his energies, and the writing of poetry frequently had to compete with the claims of scholarship, music and art. Although Hopkins was deliberate in his ascetic refusal to write poetry after he became a Jesuit in 1868, it is a mistake to think that entry into the Society of Jesus suddenly blighted a poetic career in full blossoming. Insofar as his early poems can be dated, most of them were written between 1863 and 1865, that is to say, during his first two years at Oxford. Thereafter Hopkins was engrossed in graver matters than the writing of impeccably religious verse; namely, his spiritual progress from the Anglican to the Roman Catholic Church.

2

The Convert

HOPKINS'S CHARACTER WAS a meeting-place of opposed qualities: asceticism and the love of beauty; toughness and sensitivity; quickness of sensuous response and a taste for theoretical speculation. It is possible to see something of these oppositions in his personal appearance: photographs of the nineteen-year-old Hopkins show a young man with delicate features and rather long hair carefully brushed back from a high forehead; but the nose is prominent and the mouth, though sensuous, is closed in a firm assertive line. A fellow-Jesuit who knew Hopkins in later life described him as "a slight man, with a narrow face, prominent chin and nose and—what may surprise those who know him only by his poetry—a somewhat girlish manner. He was a delightful companion, full of high spirits and innocent fun." He was also a man of marked independence of mind, at times individualistic to the point of eccentricity, who nevertheless willingly submitted himself to the highly disciplined communal life of the Society of Jesus.

Hopkins's mature poetry embodied these tensions. His love of beauty, whether in nature or in humanity, was as strong as in his Pre-Raphaelite and Aesthetic contemporaries, but he faced with greater steadfastness the inexorable fading or corruption of physical beauty. One of his finest poems, "The Leaden Echo and the Golden Echo," dramatically enacts his sense of the fragility of beauty: "Nor can you long be, what you now are, called fair." From his earliest years Hopkins had shown a strong responsiveness to individual beauty. Indeed, one family anecdote told how as a small child Gerard had been in deep distress when his younger brother was the victim of a temporarily disfiguring illness; he sobbed: "Cyril has become so ugly!" Soon after going up to Balliol Hopkins described to his mother in uncharitable but vivid terms the "full haggard hideousness" of his contemporary Martin Geldart. He found that casually observed faces could prove strangely attractive. In 1866 he wrote to Bridges about an undergraduate known only by sight whom he had unexpectedly seen in church: "His face was fascinating me last term: I generally have one fascination or another on. Sometimes I dislike the faces wh. fascinate me but sometimes much the reverse, as is the present case" (LB 8). In some painfully scrupulous confessional notes Hopkins accused himself of being too much drawn to the beauty of choristers or fellow undergraduates. Nor was it only his own sex that he found fascinating, for he also notes that he had looked too long and admiringly at a certain married woman, even to the extent of committing "adultery of the heart."

These random fascinations seem to have been as much the result of detached aesthetic attraction—Hopkins was, after all, a talented artist—as of erotic inclination. But in 1865 he met a young man to whose physical and moral beauty he was strongly drawn, who certainly involved Hopkins's emotions for a time, and who played a significant if obscure part in his spiritual development. In February of that year Digby Mackworth Dolben, a distant cousin of Bridges's, visited Oxford for a few days. He was just seventeen and had already left Eton, where his schooldays had not been harmonious; he was destined for Balliol, but needed to spend a year or so with a private tutor before taking the entrance examination. Dolben was an astonishingly precocious youth who seems to have

exemplified the tendency of Etonians—as described by the late
Cyril Connolly—to reach an absurdly early maturity and then
feel that life has no more to offer. Whether that would have
been Dolben's fate we shall never know, for at the age of
nineteen he was accidentally drowned while swimming. He left
behind a sizeable body of poetry, which Bridges eventually
edited and published, and a reputation as a devout eccentric
of compelling personality. Already, at Eton, he had got into
trouble for his extreme Anglo-Catholic tendencies, which were
inclining him towards Rome; he defied the school authorities
by persistently frequenting High Church or Roman Catholic
places of worship in the vicinity of Eton. In Bridges's words:
"he crossed himself at meals, and left his queer books about,
and behaved generally so as to make himself and his opinions
a ridiculous wonder to the boys. . . ." His attitudes were found
so insupportable that, at the age of fifteen, he was asked to
leave Eton, though he was allowed to return after some months.
Dolben then joined an order of Anglican Benedictines and fell
under the influence of Father Ignatius of Llanthony, a colourful
ecclesiastic who was attempting to revive monasticism in the
Church of England. Dolben finally left Eton for good at the
end of 1864.

In his memoir of Dolben, written many years after the deaths
of both Dolben and Hopkins, Bridges preserved only hazy
recollections of his young relation's visit to Oxford, but he
noted that "it was at this visit, and only then, that he met
Gerard Hopkins: but he must have been a good deal with
him, for Gerard conceived a high admiration for him, and
always spoke of him afterwards with great affection." The two
young men had temperamental affinities and obvious interests
in common; they were not only Anglo-Catholics but fervent
ritualists, and they shared a devotion to Savonarola. Above all,
they were both fluent writers of religious poetry, and they exchanged copies of their poems. Dolben had already contributed
poems to the High Church *Union Review*, and before long one
by Hopkins, "Barnfloor and Winepress," appeared there. The
titles of some of Dolben's poems indicate his interests: "From
the Cloister," "Good Friday," "On the Picture of an Angel by

Fra Angelico," "Flowers for the Altar." Like Hopkins he seems to have read George Herbert with some care:

> I asked for Truth—
> My doubts came in,
> And with their din
> They wearied all my youth.

He shows, too, the influence of medieval Latin hymns:

> On the silent ages breaking
> Comes the sweet Annunciation:
> The eternal Ave waking
> Changes Eva's condemnation.

Dolben is less technically adventurous than the young Hopkins, though more direct and personal, being inspired by a strong love of Christ. He is also less single-mindedly a religious poet; there is an element in his poetry, inspired by classical literature, that is distinctively pagan in a Swinburnean way:

> Sweet my sister, Queen of Hades,
> Where the quiet and the shade is,
> Of the cruel deathless ladies
> Thou art pitiful alone.

Dolben's poems are a remarkable achievement for so young a writer. They are, admittedly, less promising and individual than some of Hopkins's early work; but the comparison is unfair to Dolben, since he was nearly four years younger than Hopkins and was already dead at the age at which Hopkins began to develop as an undergraduate poet. Nevertheless, once their precocious brilliance is acknowledged, there is not much in Dolben's poems to attract a modern reader whose primary interest is in poetry rather than the development of Anglo-Catholic sensibility in mid-Victorian England. Indeed, there is a hot-house religiosity and a degree of forced emotion in Dolben's poetry that is disagreeable. Perhaps, if he had lived, he would have eventually found these adolescent compositions an embarrassment. Dolben was not a Chatterton or a Rimbaud. Yet it is easy to see why, at the time, his poems so appealed to Hopkins.

Although Hopkins never saw Dolben again after his visit to Oxford, Dolben had made a strong impression. They corresponded and exchanged poems, though Dolben was a much less assiduous letter-writer than Hopkins. In a diary entry dated 12th March 1865 Hopkins wrote: "A day of the great mercy of God." Humphry House, in his notes to Hopkins's *Journals and Papers*, suggests that this entry refers to a religious crisis connected with Dolben; it was soon afterwards that Hopkins made his first recorded confession and began his daily notes for confession (about this time he notes in his diary, as if for a purchase: "Little book for sins"). The nature of this crisis and Dolben's part in it remains obscure. It must have been a matter of intensity of devotion and scrupulosity of self-examination rather than any change of doctrinal attitudes. For the time being Hopkins was secure in his High Church allegiance; and so, indeed, was Dolben after the Romish inclinations of his Eton days, which involved him in visits to what Bridges called "a lodge of Jesuits at Old Windsor."

In April Hopkins wrote down Dolben's new address in his diary and inscribed him as "D.A.S. Mackworth Dolben," devotedly inserting Dolben's full initials even though the second and third names—Augustus Stewart—were never used. This entry is immediately followed by a poem beginning "Where art thou friend, whom I shall never see," which probably refers to Dolben. It is a sonnet, Petrarchan in form and Shakespearean in style; it is desperately obscure in sense, perhaps because of the strong but confused feelings that lay behind it.

In August Hopkins complained in a letter to Bridges that he had written "letters without end" to Dolben but "without a whiff of answer." Then, in a diary entry dated 6th November, Hopkins immediately follows an assertion of ascetic intent with an expression of joy that Dolben had at last written: "On this day by God's grace I resolved to give up all beauty until I had His leave for it;—also Dolben's letter came for which Glory to God" (J 71).

To complete the account of Hopkins and Dolben involves anticipating later events. By September 1866 Hopkins had finally resolved to enter the Catholic Church and was in correspondence with Father Newman at the Birmingham Oratory. On a visit to the Oratory Hopkins heard of Dolben's latest adventure. Whilst in Birmingham for a meeting of the Anglican Benedictine order to which he belonged, Dolben made an unannounced visit to the Oratory; Newman was away but Dolben was kindly received by Newman's friend and colleague, Father Ignatius Ryder. Dolben would have been a noticeable figure on the streets of Birmingham for, as Hopkins told Bridges: "He went in his habit without sandals, barefoot. I do not know whether it was more funny or affecting to think of." Dolben's latent inclinations towards Rome were stirring again, and they were given a further impetus when he heard of Hopkins's conversion. Early in 1867 he wrote to Newman, stating his firm intention of becoming a Catholic, adding that "Hopkins's conversion hastened the end." Dolben's father was deeply distressed—just as Hopkins's father had been a few months before—and Dolben agreed not to enter the Catholic Church until he finished at Oxford. Newman himself counselled caution, for Dolben was still very young and not at all settled in his mind. He wrote to Hopkins after Dolben's death:

He had not given up the idea of being a Catholic—but he thought he had lived on excitement, and felt he must give himself time before he could know whether he was in earnest or not. This does not seem to me a wrong frame of mind. He was up to his death careful in his devotional exercises. I never saw him [FL 407].

On 1st May 1867 Dolben came to Oxford, without telling Bridges or Hopkins, in order to sit his matriculation examination. The occasion was a disaster. His highly-strung nerves let him down; he fainted in the examination room and had to withdraw. Dolben returned for further study to the house of his tutor, the Reverend Constantine Prichard, in Lincolnshire. There, less than two months later, he was accidentally drowned whilst swimming in the river Welland. Hopkins first heard the news in July, on his return from a holiday in France. In August he wrote to Bridges:

I looked forward to meeting Dolben and his being a Catholic
more than to anything. At the same time from never having
met him but once I find it difficult to realize his death or
feel as if it were anything to me. You know there can very
seldom have happened the loss of so much beauty (in body
and mind and life) and the promise of still more as there
has been in his case—seldom, I mean, in the whole world,
for the conditions wd. not easily come together. At the same
time he had gone on in a way wh. was wholly and unhappily
irrational [LB 17].

Hopkins goes on to ask if there is to be a published collection
of Dolben's poetry—a proposal that was not in fact realized
until Bridges brought out his edition in 1911—and expresses a
hope of one day visiting the place where Dolben was buried.
The tone is sympathetically concerned but fairly detached; it
was, after all, two and a half years since Hopkins had seen
Dolben. In another letter to Bridges, later in the year, Hopkins's
tone is sharper: "It is quite true, as you say, that there was a
great want of strength in Dolben—more, of sense." On the
face of it, Hopkins's feelings about Dolben had faded almost
to indifference. Yet a quatrain by Hopkins, which can be dated
fairly precisely as early 1868, suggests that he still felt a deep
sense of loss over Dolben's death—if, indeed, the lines refer
to him (there is no other likely subject):

> Not kind! to freeze me with forecast,
> Dear grace and girder of mine and me,
> You to be gone and I lag last—
> Nor I nor heaven would have it be.

Hopkins's last reference to Dolben occurred five years later,
when he was a Jesuit scholastic. In a journal entry of 8th
September 1873 he wrote: "I received as I think a great mercy
about Dolben." It is a form of words he uses elsewhere, and
it seems to mean that he has received divine assurance of
Dolben's salvation.

I now return to Hopkins's situation in the winter of 1865–66,
when he first began to consider the possibility of becoming a

Roman Catholic. A diary entry of November 1865 reads: "Note that if ever I should leave the English Church the fact of Provost Fortescue . . . is to be got over." The point of the reference to Provost Fortescue—a well-known High Church divine—is uncertain, but the real interest of the entry is that Hopkins was at least willing to think about a change of allegiance. Meantime, he continued with ascetic practices, or at least intentions. On 23rd January 1866 he wrote:

> For Lent. No pudding on Sundays. No tea except if to keep me awake and then without sugar. Meat only once a day. No verses in Passion Week or on Fridays. No lunch or meat on Fridays. Not to sit in armchair except can work in no other way. Ash Wednesday and Good Friday bread and water [J 72].

The previous day, in a letter to Ernest Coleridge, Hopkins made an eloquent statement of his beliefs about the Incarnation, culminating in a quasi-Metaphysical paradox or conceit:

> I think that the trivialness of life is, and personally to each one, ought to be seen to be, done away with by the Incarnation—or, I shd. say the difficulty wh. the trivialness of life presents ought to be. It is one adorable point of the incredible condescension of the Incarnation (the greatness of which no saint can have ever hoped to realise) that our Lord submitted not only to the pains of life, the fasting, scourging, crucifixion etc. or the insults, as the mocking, blindfolding, spitting etc., but also to the mean and trivial accidents of humanity. It leads one naturally to rhetorical antithesis to think for instance that after making the world He shd. consent to be taught carpentering, and, being the eternal Reason, to be catechised in the theology of the Rabbins [FL 20].

This idea was amplified in Hopkins's mature poetry, where the beauty of humanity and nature does not simply reflect God as the more-or-less remote First Cause of traditional theology, but is interfused throughout with the redemptive presence of Christ himself:

> I walk, I lift up, I lift up heart, eyes,
> Down all that glory in the heavens to glean our Saviour.

In a poem called "Nondum" ("Not Yet") dated Lent 1865, Hopkins develops the more conventional theme of *Deus Absconditus*, of God silent and seemingly absent from the world, whilst man waits for a sign or a revelation. It is a competent, undistinguished piece, perhaps influenced by Tennyson's *In Memoriam*; it may, however, reveal something of Hopkins's state of mind, of one patiently waiting for a hint of divine guidance in a present difficulty.

In his journal entries for June 1866 Hopkins describes a walking tour of the west of England, made in company with one of his closest Balliol friends, William Addis, with whom he shared lodgings in Oxford that term. Addis was a keen Anglo-Catholic of somewhat emotional temperament. Their tour took them to the Catholic Benedictine monastery of St. Michael, at Belmont, near Hereford. There Hopkins and Addis had a possibly crucial meeting with one of the monks, Canon Paul Raynal. Many years later Addis wrote that Canon Raynal may well have been the first Roman Catholic priest that Hopkins had ever spoken to: "I think he made a great impression on both of us and I believe that from that time our faith in Anglicanism was really gone." Hopkins returned to St. Michael's the following year, after he had become a Catholic, to spend Holy Week and Easter.

Conversion is a mysterious process and one can only speculate about the factors that impelled Hopkins from Anglicanism to Roman Catholicism in the summer of 1866. But if the encounter with Canon Raynal was as decisive as Addis claimed, its effect was probably to reinforce existing doubts and dissatisfactions in Hopkins's mind rather than to accomplish a sudden transformation of his allegiance. In September, when his decision had been firmly made, he told another friend, the Reverend E. W. Urquhart: "the silent conviction that I was to become a Catholic has been present to me for a year perhaps, as strongly, in spite of my resistance to it, when it formed itself into words as if I had already determined it" (FL 27).

Hopkins's conversion was not in any obvious sense an emotional affair, and it was certainly not a response to the supposedly greater aesthetic appeal of the Church of Rome. As he told his father on the eve of his reception into the Catholic Church: "I am surprised you shd. say fancy and aesthetic tastes have led me to my present state of mind; these wd. be better satisfied in the Church of England, for bad taste is always meeting one in the accessories of Catholicism" (FL 93). As an Anglo-Catholic Hopkins would already have embraced all the doctrines and practices of the Roman Catholic Church, except the one point of papal supremacy. If anything, the Anglo-Catholics tended to greater extremes of private devotion than were approved of by the ecclesiastical discipline of the Roman Church, such as their passion for fasting and, in some cases, flagellation.

Like all the Tractarians Hopkins would have regarded himself as wholly Catholic, though after his conversion he always uses "Catholic" to mean "Roman Catholic." In leaving the Church of England Hopkins was driven by the arguments about authority that had set Newman on the same path twenty years earlier. The arguments concerned the essential nature of the Church of England, and they had continued unabated since the high Tractarian days of the late thirties and early forties. Did the Church of England possess the true Apostolic succession or was it merely a schismatic body, broken off at the Reformation from the true Catholic Church founded by St. Peter, whose present successor still reigned in Rome as Vicar of Christ? Those Anglicans who, like Newman and Hopkins and several hundred others in the intervening years, came to the firm conclusion that the Anglican claims to the Apostolic succession were historically unjustified had no alternative but to join the Church of Rome, whatever the psychological and cultural obstacles. Other Anglicans, like Pusey and Liddon, were equally convinced that the Church of England was indeed the Catholic Church in England and that the Roman claims had no justification. Others, again, could not make up their minds and sometimes spent a whole lifetime in anguished uncertainty, even to the extent of moving from one Church to another and back again, like John Moore Capes, editor of *The Rambler*, and Thomas Arnold, junior, later to be Hopkins's colleague as Professor of English at University College, Dublin.

It was a perennial problem for the Tractarian camp that, after having encouraged their adherents to be as Catholic as possible, many of them found they could be even more Catholic in the Roman allegiance. This constant defection was a particular cause of bitterness to Pusey, who found himself having to fight on too many fronts at the same time: against unbelief, the Broad Church, the Low Church and Rome itself. Thus, Hopkins's conversion was by no means an isolated event, though it may well have been felt as a particularly keen loss by the Oxford Anglo-Catholics because of Hopkins's personal and intellectual qualities. In the summer of 1866 one of his acquaintances, Henry William Challis, a mathematician and a member of Merton College, was received into the Catholic Church; and his own reception in October was immediately preceded by that of no less than three of his friends: William Addis, William Garrett and Alexander Wood; largely, it seems, as a response to Hopkins's own decision. These young men appear to have been received into the Catholic Church in a fairly casual way, with inadequate preparation by modern standards. There must, indeed, have been an element of collective emotion to these conversions, though Hopkins himself insisted that his own conversion was a matter of logic and hard reasoning; as he told Liddon soon after his reception: "I can hardly believe anyone ever became a Catholic because two and two make four more fully than I have." It is hardly surprising that not all these conversions of impressionable undergraduates endured. Challis left the Catholic Church after only a few years, while Addis, after having become a priest and helping to compile an authoritative *Catholic Dictionary*, finally gave up Catholicism in 1888, greatly to Hopkins's distress.

The first clear sign of Hopkins's conversion occurs in a journal entry dated 17th July:

It was this night I believe but possibly the next that I saw clearly the impossibility of staying in the Church of England but resolved to say nothing to anyone till three months are over, that is the end of the Long, and then of course to take no step till after my Degree.

Hopkins did not keep either of these resolutions. He was at that time on holiday with two Oxford friends, William Garrett and William Macfarlane, staying in a farmhouse near Horsham, Sussex, of which Hopkins remarked with characteristic aesthetic fastidiousness: "The farm is as ugly as can be but the country very pretty." The holiday was punctuated with a good deal of church-going, for all three young men were conspicuously devout: Garrett, soon to become a Catholic himself, was a member of the Brotherhood of the Holy Trinity, and Macfarlane was shortly to be ordained in the Church of England. Hopkins's spiritual struggles may have affected his demeanour, for Macfarlane complained in his diary that Hopkins had been rather disagreeable, and he and Garrett had "a serious talk with Hopkins about his manners etc." In the end Hopkins was unable to keep his secret; Macfarlane noted in his diary: "Walked out with Hopkins and he confided to me his fixed intention of going over to Rome. I did not attempt to argue with him as his grounds did not admit of argument" (FL 397). Hopkins's own entry for that day, 24th July, is terser: "Spoke to Macfarlane, foolishly." There is a pleasant record of this holiday in the group photograph reproduced in the *Further Letters*, taken, according to Macfarlane's diary, by a photographer at Horsham at 4 p.m. on 27th July. The picture was taken out of doors; the three young men, though only twenty-two, have the distinctly middle-aged look of Victorian undergraduates, particularly Macfarlane, the only one of the three to be seated, a grave personage with a full black beard. Hopkins looks a little younger, a short, slight, dapper figure, with well brushed hair, holding his hat and cane at a careful angle.

From Horsham Hopkins travelled to join his family on holiday at Shanklin in the Isle of Wight. He regretted having spoken to Garrett and Macfarlane of his decision and resolved to tell no-one else until what he judged to be an appropriate moment. But in a letter to Bridges of 4th August he refers in a pointed way to the recent conversion of Challis, obliquely revealing something of his own preoccupations:

> He never had much belief in the Church of England, and his going over in itself wd. prove as little as any conversion could ever do against it since he never used the same strictness in practices (such as fasting) as most of our acquaintance would, but on the other hand if its effect is to make him a strict catholic and to destroy his whimsies, that would say something [LB 3].

It was a full summer for Hopkins. After his holiday in the Isle of Wight he had arranged to visit Bridges at Rochdale, Lancashire; a further inducement—though not in fact realised—was the possible presence there of Dolben. But first, in Hampstead on 28th August, Hopkins took a decisive step. He wrote to Newman at the Birmingham Oratory, tentatively asking for an interview, saying that if it were convenient he could call and see Newman later that week in the course of travelling north to Rochdale. His mind was totally made up about the necessity of becoming a Catholic, but the necessity "coming upon me suddenly has put me into painful confusion about my immediate duty in my circumstances." Although he had never met Newman, his friend Addis had, and he hoped this might serve as sufficient introduction. Newman was away when Hopkins's letter arrived but he wrote in the middle of September, readily agreeing to see him at any convenient time, and the meeting was arranged for 20th September, on Hopkins's way back from Lancashire.

It was not surprising that Hopkins should seek to see Newman: a young Oxford convert from Tractarianism might well want to seek advice from one who had followed the same path in the 1840s. Any hesitation in Hopkins's letter may have arisen because Newman was now a nationally famous figure after the years of obscurity that had followed his entry into the Catholic Church. The publication of *Apologia Pro Vita Sua* in 1864 had brought him unaccustomed celebrity as man and writer; he was admired by many readers who had no sympathy at all for Roman Catholicism. What is astonishing is the total absence of any reference to Newman's book in Hopkins's undergraduate diaries or letters. It would certainly have been discussed at Oxford, and it seems unlikely that Hopkins, so widely read and so aware of contemporary issues and arguments, did not read the *Apologia,* or at least know about it. But there is no evidence that he did.

At Rochdale Hopkins and Bridges read classical texts together. Or at least they tried to, until Bridges found he could no longer cope with Hopkins's method of work: "He was so punctilious about the text, and so enjoyed loitering over the difficulties, that I foresaw we should never get through, and broke off from him to go my own way."[1] Until the very end of his visit, Hopkins said nothing about his conversion, partly, it seems, because he did not want to offend Bridges's stepfather, the Reverend Dr. Molesworth, vicar of Rochdale. Although it was a period of anxiety for Hopkins, awaiting his meeting with Newman, he insisted to Bridges afterwards that "it gives me more delight to think of the time at Rochdale than any other time whatever that I can remember." He told his father something similar, in the painful correspondence they exchanged just before Hopkins entered the Catholic Church: "It is possible even to be very sad and very happy at once and the time that I was with Bridges, when my anxiety came to its height, was I believe the happiest fortnight of my life" (FL 95). Hopkins was particularly grateful to Bridges for his kindness and forbearance during his stay.

On 20th September Hopkins finally met Newman and was treated with exemplary courtesy and consideration. In the perspective of cultural history we can now see it as a significant moment: the first meeting of the two greatest Catholic writers in English of the nineteenth century. Back at the family home in Hampstead Hopkins wrote at once to Bridges his impressions of the meeting: "Dr. Newman was most kind, I mean in the very best sense, for his manner is not that of solicitous kindness but genial and almost, so to speak, unserious. And if I

[1] Robert Bridges, ed., *The Poems of Digby Mackworth Dolben* (London: 1915), p. ci.

may say so, he was so sensible" (LB 5). It was hardly an
unusual situation for Newman; at the age of sixty-five he had
had many years' experience, both as Anglican and Catholic,
helping young men with religious problems. He satisfied himself that Hopkins was in earnest and that his arguments for
wanting to become a Catholic were well thought out and held
water. Having done so, he told Hopkins that he could be received into the Church in the near future, once he had settled
matters with his parents. This last question was at the heart
of Hopkins's anxiety. He was of age and did not need their
formal consent, but he knew that his parents shared the customary English prejudices against the Church of Rome and
would be appalled at his decision. He resolved to put off telling
them until the very point of his reception, which he had arranged with Newman to take place early in the autumn term.
Hopkins desired, in effect, to present his parents with a *fait
accompli*, which, though not at all considerate from their point
of view, made good sense from his. He wished to spare himself for as long as possible a formidable combination of emotional pressure and would-be persuasive arguments, for the
Hopkins parents were both devoted and articulate Anglicans.
Already several of his friends knew of his decision—Garrett,
Macfarlane, Bridges—and he now wrote telling another close
friend, E. W. Urquhart, a young clergyman of High Church
leanings who was curate at the church of St. Philip and St.
James in Oxford. Urquhart had for some time been entertaining doubts about the Anglican position. He seemed to be in
much the same predicament that Hopkins had just emerged
from, and the new convert assumed that it only needed a little
pressure and argument to bring Urquhart into the fold. So he
subjected the wavering Urquhart to several stiff letters of
sharp proseletysing polemic, setting out what were for Hopkins
the irrefutable arguments for the Roman case. (Hopkins's capacity for fine ratiocination is likely to surprise those who
know him only as a poet, or who think that such intellectual
operations are irreconcilable with the practice of poetry.) But
argument can go only a limited way in such matters, even
though a young man of fine and well-trained intellect, with

a burning case to argue and little experience of the world, might find that hard to believe. Newman, with a long experience of such situations, would have had fewer expectations. For whatever reason, Hopkins failed. Urquhart stayed where he was and indeed remained in the Anglican communion until his death in 1916. Writing to Urquhart on 24th September, Hopkins said that so far few of his friends knew of his conversion, but added ominously: "One of my brothers knows it; he forced it from me by questions." This, indeed, is what happens in closely-knit families; but Hopkins's parents were not yet told.

Meantime, however, Hopkins was caught up in a practical distraction of an almost farcical kind. When he left Rochdale Bridges had entrusted to him a slightly complicated errand in London. Bridges wanted to present a communion vessel of a specific kind—a flagon with an ornamental stopper—to the church of Thorndon in Suffolk, where his brother-in-law was rector. There were many possible suppliers of such objects in London and Hopkins agreed to make the purchase; he also offered, if nothing suitable could be found in stock, to design the stopper himself. In the event, he had great trouble in discovering the right kind of shop, but was finally directed to a dealer and manufacturer called Mr. Keith who lived at a remote and unfashionable address off the City Road; "an incredible place to live at and hard to find," remarked Hopkins with the innocent superiority of an inhabitant of Hampstead. He was not impressed with what Keith had in stock, he told Bridges in a letter of 8th October, illustrated with neat sketches of a flagon and stoppers; he suggested one ought to be designed specially. The problem was that although Hopkins was willing and able to design a stopper, a whole bottle was beyond his powers. But he included possible designs for a stopper in his letter. A further visit to the shop was unsatisfactory because of the absence of Mr. Keith, though more possible designs for a stopper were produced. Hopkins showed throughout intense anxiety not to spend more of Bridges's money than was strictly necessary. The negotiation was still incomplete when Hopkins had to go back to Oxford for the autumn term, but during the Christmas vacation he faithfully returned to Keith's, and wrote to Bridges about the latest development. The whole business clearly preyed on his mind. In the end, though, the flagon and stopper were completed and duly sent to Thorndon church where they were in use for many years. The episode is trivial, but Hopkins's handling of the business demonstrates his obsessive punctiliousness in practical matters and his moral scrupulosity about making decisions. It was precisely this combination of qualities that made the marking of examination papers so anguishing when, in later years, Hopkins was a University Professor in Dublin.

Hopkins resolved not to tell his parents about his conversion until he was back in Oxford, and then to do so by letter. He did, however, write from Hampstead to his former guide and confessor, Dr. Pusey; the letter has not survived but it appears that Hopkins told Pusey of his decision to become a Catholic and asked to see him. Pusey declined, and Hopkins wrote again. Pusey was unmoved, and his letter of 10th October harshly breaks off relations with Hopkins. It has too often happened, he said, that intending converts to Rome—Pusey uses the then-current word "pervert"—have wished to see him in a face-saving way, so they can say to others, particularly their relations: " 'I have seen Dr. P., and he has failed to satisfy me,' whereas they knew very well that they meant not to be satisfied, that they came with a fixed purpose not to be satisfied. This is merely to waste my time, and create the impression that I have nothing to say." Pusey was probably right on this point but his tone is little short of brutal. He concludes by telling Hopkins: "You have a heavy responsibility. Those who will gain by what you seem determined to do, will be the unbelievers" (FL 400).

Hopkins's letter from Oxford to his father was delivered at Oak Hill, Hampstead, on the evening of Saturday, 13th October. He told his parents of his decision, and insisted that it was based on profound and thorough consideration of the matter. The letter came as a sudden and devastating blow to them. Thereafter followed a week of urgent letter-writing between several different parties. Hopkins's parents both wrote shocked, incredulous letters, begging him to reconsider or at least delay his decision until after he had taken his degree. So efficient was the postal service of those days that Hopkins received their letters on Monday, 15th October. The same day he wrote to Newman: "I have been up at Oxford just long enough to have heard fr. my father and mother in return for my letter announcing my conversion. Their answers are terrible: I cannot read them twice. If you will pray for them and me just now I shall be deeply thankful" (FL 29). Although three months earlier he had thought he would finish his time at Oxford before making a final decision, that no longer seemed possible. However much his parents urged delay he could no longer consider it: "since it is impossible to wait as long as they wish it seems to me useless to wait at all." He wished, in short, to travel to Birmingham and be received into the Catholic Church by Newman as soon as possible. Newman's reply, dated the 18th, was brief but reassuring: "It is not wonderful that you should not be able to take so great a step without trouble and pain." He invited Hopkins to Birmingham on the following Sunday.

At the same time others were attempting, even at the last moment, to pull Hopkins back from the brink. On the 15th Manley Hopkins wrote to Canon Liddon, whom he had never met, but whom he knew Gerard revered and admired. He described the appalling effect of his son's letter—"this blow is so deadly & great that we have not yet recovered from the first shock of it"—and he appealed to Liddon to exert all his influence to prevent Gerard from taking this irrevocable step. Manley Hopkins's letter, distressed but lucid, shows that he could scarcely believe that his son was in his right mind: Gerard's judgment was still immature, and however much he might think he had reasoned himself to his present situation, in reality "he is following impulses, even fancies, but with some present obstinacy." Manley rises to a pitch of impressive eloquence in his final appeal to Liddon:

> save him from throwing a pure life and a somewhat unusual intellect away in the cold limbo which Rome assigns to her

English converts. The deepness of our distress, the shattering
of our hopes & the foreseen estrangement which must happen, are my excuse for writing to you so freely & so press-
ingly; but even these motives do not weigh with us in
comparison of our pity for our dear son, and distress at
the future life to which he is in such danger of committing
himself [FL 435].

Liddon had already heard from an Oxford acquaintance about
Hopkins's conversion and was almost as disturbed by the
news as Manley Hopkins. He was unavoidably detained in
Bristol all that week, so could not make any personal appeal to
Hopkins, but he wrote to him four times in as many days,
begging him to reconsider or at least delay; his letters contained a combination of the familiar Anglican arguments about
ecclesiastical authority and intense moral persuasion. They
were written in affectionate terms that contrasted with Pusey's
harshness. But Liddon seems from the beginning to have been
doubtful of achieving anything: perhaps he knew Hopkins's
obstinate character too well.

On the 16th October Hopkins began a long reply to his
father's letter and finished it the following day. The tone is,
as Manley complained, "hard and cold"; understandably, perhaps, since Hopkins could only cope with his situation by
deliberately fending off his parents' emotional pressure. Hopkins traces the recent development of his religious opinions and
insists that his conversion was not at all a matter of "fancy and
aesthetic tastes." His respect for Pusey and Liddon would have
kept him in the Church of England if anything would, but
"when that influence gave way everything was gone." In parts
of the letter Hopkins masks his personal emotion with a kind
of bleak punctilio:

You are so kind as not to forbid me your house, to which
I have no claim, on condition, if I understand, that I promise
not to try to convert my brothers and sisters. Before I can
promise this I must get permission, wh. I have no doubt
will be given. Of course this promise will not apply after

they come of age. Whether after my reception you will still speak as you do now I cannot tell [FL 94].

Hopkins ends the letter by applying moral and emotional pressure of his own. He tells his father that if only he and his mother would put themselves in the right frame of mind and pray to Christ with sufficient devotion they, too, might see the light and take the same path as he has, thereby avoiding all estrangements. It was a suggestion that Manley found peculiarly outrageous. His reply, of which a draft survives, is a pained accusation that Hopkins is following his private judgment and has not prayed for sufficient guidance; the underlying assumption is that no-one who wishes to leave the Church of England could really be in good faith. He also accuses Gerard of intending to be received into the Church of Rome without telling his parents at all until a friend dissuaded him, and concludes with an outburst that must have been peculiarly painful to the recipient: "O Gerard my darling boy are you indeed gone from me?" The last of the letters that survive from that crucial week of Hopkins's life is one written to his mother, on Saturday 20th October. If the manner is less hard than in the previous letter to his father, it is still an argumentative letter, engaged in making points in a way that could hardly have soothed his mother's distress. Yet this, too, was a means of checking his own considerable emotional disturbance, which is very apparent by the end of the letter. The last two paragraphs are worth quoting in full:

I was never going to be received without warning you, though I was going to give you the warning only at the last. In this I have no doubt I was wrong. In not warning you of my state of mind long ago I strongly think I was perfectly right. But if I was wrong in both cases, I of course thought only of the way wh. I believed wd. give you the least pain: indeed if you can think I did otherwise it wd. be useless of me to assure you of it.

I am to be received into the church tomorrow at Birmingham by Dr. Newman. It is quite the best that any hopes should be ended quickly, since otherwise they wd. only have made the pain longer. Until then the comforts you take are delusive, after it they will be real. And even for me it is almost a matter of necessity, for every new letter I get breaks me down afresh, and this cd. not go on. Your letters, wh. show the utmost fondness, suppose none on my part and the more you think me hard and cold and that I repel and throw you off the more I am helpless not to write as if it were true. In this way I have no relief. You might believe that I suffer too. I am your very loving son [FL 99–100].

When the letter arrived at Hampstead on Monday, 22nd October, Hopkins was already a Roman Catholic, and the brief but painful episode was closed. To a modern reader it is a reminder of the weight of parental power in even an enlightened Victorian family: it was taken for granted that a young man of twenty-two, with three years' university education behind him, was simply not capable of taking a major decision in life for himself. It shows, too, the pressure of religious prejudice that the convert to Rome had to encounter.

Hopkins settled down at Oxford for the final year of the Greats course. There was a further ripple of the excitements and debates leading up to his reception into the Catholic Church in the form of a long letter to Canon Liddon, dated 7th November. Here Hopkins sets down the reasons for his conversion, insisting that it was not a matter of "personal illumination" but of intellectual conviction. The letter shows Hopkins at his most characteristically argumentative, though it concludes with an expression of continuing affection and regard for Liddon. As a Catholic, Hopkins was now in an anomalous position at Oxford. The Roman Catholic hierarchy did not permit Catholics to attend Oxford or Cambridge, fearing the heretical religious environment. This restriction was to be a cause of bitter dispute in the Catholic community in England almost until the end of the century, when Catholics were finally permitted to attend the ancient universities. Opinions varied about the situation of undergraduates who were converted whilst at the university. Archbishop Manning followed a strict line. When he confirmed Alexander Wood in a London church in the autumn of 1866 he told him that of course there could be no question of his returning to Oxford, though Wood chose to disregard this injunction. Newman, on the other hand, took it for granted that Hopkins would return to Balliol for his final year; indeed, assured him that his first duty was to get as good a degree as possible. The Oxford establishment, for its part, did not make life easy for Catholics at the university. As a wholly Anglican institution it obliged all undergraduates to attend chapel. Balliol, a liberal college, readily granted Hopkins a dispensation, but he found that attending Sunday Mass in Oxford produced problems. At that time the only Catholic place of worship in the city was the small chapel of St. Ignatius. On more than one occasion when Hopkins and Wood had been to Mass there they had their names taken by university officials and were fined by the Junior Proctor for the offence of attending a Roman rather than an Anglican service. In the words of a modern Jesuit: "thus Hopkins joined late in the day the band of Oxford Recusants which began with Cardinal Allen, Persons, and Campion."[2] But such attempts to impose ecclesiastical uniformity by legal sanctions were already archaic and before long broke down altogether.

Following the distressing correspondence with his parents in October, Hopkins believed that they might no longer welcome his presence at home. He mentioned his fears to Newman, who invited him to spend the Christmas vacation at the Birmingham Oratory. Happily, Hopkins's anxieties were groundless and, as in previous years, he spent Christmas at Hampstead, though he did go to the Birmingham Oratory for a week's retreat in January 1867. Before Christmas Newman wrote to him, with characteristic urbanity: "I want to see you for the pleasure of seeing you—but, besides that, I think it good that a recent convert should pass some time in a religious house, to get into Catholic ways—though a week is not long enough for that purpose" (FL 406). Following this visit to Birmingham, when the question of Hopkins's future employment was dis-

---

[2] J. H. Crehan, "New Light on Hopkins," *The Month*, October 1953.

cussed, Newman invited him to become a teacher at the Oratory School. Newman had founded this school in 1859 as a Catholic equivalent of an English public school; it employed lay teachers and avoided the monastic atmosphere of the Catholic schools run by religious orders. Hopkins hesitated. He had some doubts, not without foundation, of his capability as a teacher; but Newman, already aware of Hopkins's reputation at Balliol as an outstanding classicist, regarded his young convert as a distinguished potential addition to the school and was gently but firmly persuasive. Before long Hopkins accepted, and it was arranged that he would begin his duties when the new scholastic year started in September.

Hopkins devoted his remaining months at Oxford to intensive work for his final examinations and altogether gave up writing poetry. In the spring Jowett, who thought of Hopkins as a star pupil, put him through a two-day examination; "a most trying thing" he called it in a letter to his mother. He spent Easter at St. Michael's Priory, Hereford, and after a brief visit to Hampstead was back in Oxford for the summer term. The melancholy he felt at approaching the end of his four years in that insidiously beautiful environment was emphasised by his discontent at the extensive rebuilding of Balliol then under way. The medieval buildings were being replaced by smart neo-Gothic structures; "There seems to be no conservative spirit at work at all in the buildings that are to be," Hopkins told his mother. His dissatisfaction with the changes has been echoed by a modern architectural critic, H. M. Colvin: "It is difficult to find much to admire in Waterhouse's baronial front to Broad Street or in Salvin's Tower at the junction of the old hall and library. What they replaced was of no special interest, but it had the merit of being venerable, authentic, and modest. . . ."[3]

Meantime the final examinations were approaching. Later that year, when Bridges was in the same situation, Hopkins wrote to him: "Is not the thought of Greats like a mill-stone round your neck now? It was to me." But, whatever anxiety he

[3] H. M. Colvin, *Ackermann's Oxford* (London: 1954), p. 14.

felt during the run-up period, Hopkins gave the triumphant performance that everyone expected. Not only did he get a first-class degree, but Professor Wilson, one of the examiners, told Bridges: " 'for form' he was by far the best man in the first class."[4] Hopkins thanked his friends for their congratulations, showed himself tactfully pleased or disappointed about the results of his contemporaries and then, on 10th July 1867, left for a week in Paris. His companion on this visit was Basil Poutiatine, or Putyatin, a recent graduate of Christ Church, who was an acquaintance rather than a particularly close friend. Poutiatine's father, whom they met in Paris, was a Russian admiral and former naval attaché in London. This short holiday was Hopkins's first trip to the Continent since he had visited Germany with his father in 1860. Its purpose was to visit the great Exposition, one of the glories of the Second Empire, which attempted to rival the famous London Exhibition of 1851. In Paris Hopkins was a busy tourist. As well as paying several visits to the Exposition he went to Nôtre Dame, to the Louvre and the Madeleine. He also saw one of the more up-to-date sights of Paris, Nadar's famous balloon, later to achieve a special celebrity during the siege by the Prussians in 1871. In the Bois de Boulogne Hopkins made some rather disapproving notes on the vegetation: "In B. de B. noticed the thinness of French foliage, weakness of the general type of the tree, and naked shrub-like growth of the oaks" (J 148). A rough return passage from Dieppe to Newhaven provided the opportunity for a Ruskinian description of the state of the sea:

Got soaked with spray and cheeks frosted with brine, but I saw the waves well. In the sunlight they were green-blue, flinty sharp, and rucked in straight lines by the wind; under their forelocks the most beautiful bottle-green beam, as bright as any gems; when the wave had passed this same part—upon the turned-over plait of the crest—neighboured by and sometimes broken by foam, looked like chrysoprase [J 178].

---

[4] Bridges, *op. cit.*, p. ci.

He returned to Hampstead to find a letter with news of Dolben's death. The next few weeks Hopkins spent uneventfully at home; he visited an exhibition of foreign paintings with his Aunt Kate; he went for walks in the rural surroundings of Hampstead with his younger brothers; he sketched and carefully noted the appearances of things in his journal. He was, in fact, filling in time before beginning work as a teacher at the Oratory School. He had been expecting an invitation from Pater to visit him at Sidmouth in Devon, but no word came from his former tutor. He did, however, go to Devon in August as the guest of E. W. Urquhart, now a curate at the parish church of Bovey Tracy; Hopkins was still trying to argue Urquhart into the Catholic Church, but this did not affect the friendship. In Devon Hopkins made notes on nature and on the architecture of the local churches. Then, on 10th September, he travelled directly from Devon to Birmingham to begin a new life at the Oratory.

Although Newman had assured him: "You will not find your work here hard," Hopkins did, in fact, find the life of a resident schoolmaster both hard and time-consuming, particularly after the leisurely life he had lived since graduating from Oxford. He had to get up at 6.15, and the whole of the day thereafter was filled with teaching and preparation, not to mention participating in the boys' games of hockey or football. The boys he found likeable enough, though. Writing to Urquhart at the end of September, he gives a strong impression of making the best of things:

I feel as if they were all my children, a notion encouraged by their innocence and backwardness. They never swear beyond Con-found you, you young fool, and that only one of them. The masters' table appears to be the dregs of Great Britain, indeed one of us is a Dutchman but I cannot spell his name: when I say dregs I only mean that they come fr. all quarters indiscriminately and I include myself: it is sweepings, not dregs I mean. They are nice souls and one of them, a very young man, I like particularly [FL 44].

It was a gentler and less strenuous atmosphere than the one Hopkins had known as a boy at Highgate School, though he did injure his ankle in a game of football. As the autumn wore on he fitted into the repetitive routine of teaching. His journal, so full and observant during his recent holiday in Devon, dwindled to a series of brief notes on the weather. Later in the term he was pleased by the arrival of his Oxford acquaintance, Henry Challis, who had joined the teaching staff. Hopkins took considerable pleasure in music; Newman was a proficient amateur violinist, and played quartets with the music master and two of the boys; before long Hopkins started learning the violin, too. As in previous years he spent the Christmas vacation with his family at Hampstead. In London there were outings to plays and concerts, and a round of family visits. After one of these he noted in his journal the idiosyncrasies of speech of his infant cousin Mildred: an interesting re-emergence of Hopkins's always latent preoccupation with language; an anticipation, too, of James Joyce's representation of childish speech in the opening of *Portrait of the Artist*.

Back at Birmingham after the vacation Hopkins felt that life as a schoolmaster was becoming insupportable. Writing to Alexander Baillie on 12th February 1868, he gave a revealing account of his complex state of mind:

I must say that I am very anxious to get away from this place. I have become very weak in health and do not seem to recover myself here or likely to do so. Teaching is very burdensome, especially when you have much of it: I have. I have not much time and almost no energy—for I am always tired—to do anything on my own account. I put aside that one sees and hears nothing and nobody here. Very happily Challis of Merton is now here; else the place were without reservation "damned, shepherd." (This is not swearing.) I ought to make the exception that the boys are very nice indeed. I am expecting to take orders and soon, but I wish it to be secret till it comes about. Besides that it is the happiest and best way it practically is the only one. You know

I once wanted to be a painter. But even if I could I wd. not I think, now, for the fact is that the higher and more attractive parts of the art put a strain upon the passions which I shd. think it unsafe to encounter. I want to write still and as a priest I very likely can do that too, not so freely as I shd. have liked, e.g. nothing or little in the verse way, but no doubt what wd. best serve the cause of my religion. But if I am a priest it will cause my mother, or she says it will, great grief and this preys on my mind very much and makes the near prospect quite black. The general result is that I am perfectly reckless about things that I shd. otherwise care about, uncertain as I am whether in a few months I may not be shut up in a cloister, and this state of mind, though it is painful coming to, when reached gives a great and real sense of freedom [FL 231–32].

This passage faintly anticipates the letters Hopkins wrote from his Dublin exile some twenty years later. There are the same complaints about his health and the insupportable burdens of teaching and the lack of time, and the same disquieting note of bitterness. Already the dominant features of his temperament were apparent: he was a man of great intellectual gifts, who had much difficulty in putting them to systematic use in an institutional context. Hence, no doubt, the reputation he was later to acquire in the Jesuit order as a brilliant but difficult man. Hopkins's temperamental problems were underlined by his extreme sensitivity to environment; Birmingham had evidently become uncongenial to him, just as Dublin would. Indeed, the one place where he was to feel really happy and at home was the Jesuit house at St. Beuno's in Flintshire. But in 1868 Hopkins was still a young man, encountering the major decisions of life. The sense of inner struggle that the above quotation gives is, again, characteristic. The decision to become a priest could hardly have surprised his friends. Indeed, before his conversion, Manley Hopkins had assumed that his son was destined for the Anglican ministry, given his conspicuous piety. The letter to Baillie shows, too, Hopkins's painful scrupulosity about the practice of art and poetry; the conscious abandonment of poetry was not, as is sometimes assumed, a result of his decision to become a Jesuit but preceded it by several months. It may not be an accident that the last piece of Hopkins's verse surviving from his early years, and written at about the same time as this letter, is the cryptic quatrain seemingly in memory of Dolben.

Hopkins discussed his difficulties with Newman, who responded with his customary understanding and gentleness. It was agreed that Hopkins would stay at the Oratory until Easter, when he would finally decide what to do: "we shall be able to manage matters whether you stay, or we have the mishap to lose you." In April, during Holy Week, there was a retreat at the Oratory conducted by a Jesuit, Father Henry Coleridge, a convert from Anglicanism and a close friend of Newman's. Father Coleridge was probably the first Jesuit Hopkins had met and the encounter could have been crucial. The retreat ended with High Mass on Maundy Thursday, and on Easter Sunday, 12th April, Newman preached. On 15th April Hopkins wrote in his journal: "Fine but rather dim. Left the Oratory. To Hampstead." Another phase of his life was over; meantime, the parental home continued to provide a welcome resting place.

Within the next few weeks Hopkins made several rapid but firm decisions that decided the course of his future life. On 27th April he went into retreat at the Jesuit house at Roehampton, a few miles to the south-west of London. Back at Hampstead on 7th May he wrote in his journal: "Home, after having decided to be a priest and religious but still doubtful between St. Benedict and St. Ignatius" (J 168). At that time, and for many years to come, highly educated converts who became priests tended to join the prestigious orders of Jesuits or Benedictines rather than the ordinary clergy. The retreat at Roehampton might have confirmed in Hopkins an attraction to the Jesuits first implanted by Father Coleridge; on the other hand, his visits to the Benedictines of Belmont Abbey, Hereford, in 1866 and 1867 had been both happy and influential. Within a day or so he definitely decided to become a Jesuit, despite a sense that life in that order might be harder than among the Benedictines.

He wrote to tell Newman of his decision, and he replied with urbane congratulations, saying that he was "surprised and glad" at the news. It was, he assured Hopkins, the right thing for him: "Don't call 'the Jesuit discipline hard,' it will bring you to heaven. The Benedictines would not have suited you." On 19th May Hopkins was interviewed by Father Alfred Weld, Provincial of the English Province of the Society of Jesus, to ascertain his suitability for the Jesuit novitiate. Meanwhile he had made another important and even dramatic personal decision. A terse journal entry for 11th May notes the "slaughter of the innocents" and refers back to earlier, equally cryptic entries. As Humphry House convincingly argued, there is strong circumstantial evidence that the "slaughter of the innocents" was the destruction by Hopkins of the poems he had written up to that time. The earlier journal entries suggest that he had been contemplating such an act for a long time. Writing to Bridges in August 1868 he says he has burnt his poems: "I saw they wd. interfere with my state and vocation." It seems, though, to have been an act of personal and symbolic significance rather than a determined effort to erase all traces of his poetic activity. He was well aware that Bridges had kept many of his poems in manuscript and he sent Bridges corrected versions of some of them after the "slaughter." But henceforth he wrote no more poetry—apart from "two or three little presentation pieces which occasion called for"—until "The Wreck of the *Deutschland*" in 1875.

On 28th May Hopkins went to Oxford to take his degree. There he saw Swinburne and met Simeon Solomon, then at the height of his celebrity as a Pre-Raphaelite painter, though a few years later he was disgraced and imprisoned. He also made several unsuccessful efforts to see Canon Liddon. Back in London on 30th May he found a letter from Father Weld accepting him for the Society of Jesus; a few days later he told Liddon in a farewell letter: "I am going to enter the Jesuit noviciate at Roehampton: I do not think there is another prospect so bright in the world" (FL 49). Liddon can hardly have been delighted at the news, though he may have appreciated his former protégé's punctilious consideration in informing him. In a long and argumentative letter to Urquhart, whom he was still trying to coax into the Catholic Church, Hopkins said of his decision: "Since I made up my mind to this I have enjoyed the first complete peace of mind I have ever had. I am quite surprised—not that on reflection it is surprising—at the kind and contented way my parents have come to take the prospect" (FL 51). He would not enter the novitiate until September and he spent the rest of June in his usual vacation activities: walks in the country around Hampstead and going to concerts and exhibitions in London. On 17th June he lunched with Pater, then visited Simeon Solomon's studio and went on to the Academy.

On 3rd July Hopkins left England for a walking holiday in Switzerland. His companion was Edward Bond, formerly an undergraduate at St. John's, Oxford; Bond was evidently a close friend of Hopkins at this time, though he is a shadowy figure in the journal and letters; he was not conspicuous in the Oxford circles that Hopkins frequented, nor was he noted for any strong religious interests. In 1868 the Alps were very popular with English visitors. Such distinguished men as Edward Whymper, Leslie Stephen and John Tyndall had developed the sport—or science—of mountaineering, and in the past few years most of the Alpine peaks had been conquered. For Hopkins there were other attractions. His master Ruskin had been captivated by the Alps from boyhood, and had devoted many pages of *Modern Painters* to describing and speculating about them in a strange combination of religious reverie and scientific rigour. In Switzerland Hopkins wrote very full accounts of what he saw in his journal, in contrast to the perfunctory entries he had been making for the past year or so. There was much to describe; Hopkins and Bond climbed several of the lesser peaks, no doubt by easy routes and with the assistance of guides; nevertheless, it was a strenuous undertaking for so physically frail a young man, though Hopkins seems to have been none the worse for it. Once, at the foot of the Matterhorn, they fell in with the famous scientist and Alpine explorer Professor Tyndall, preparing to set off on his third—and this time successful—attempt on the peak (it had been first climbed by Edward Whymper, three years before). It was only a brief meeting, though Hopkins said that Tyndall was kind to them and prescribed appropriate treatment for Bond, who was unwell. Six years later Hopkins read with critical interest Tyndall's Presidential Address to the British Association and recalled their meeting in a letter to his mother: "I fear he must be called an atheist but he is not a shameless one: I wish he might come round." There was something symbolic in this passing encounter of two contrasting Victorian figures: the sacramental poet and the rationalistic man of science.

Hopkins responded to the mountains with awe and enthusiasm, as Ruskin had done. Indeed, he saw the Alps very much through Ruskin's eyes; as well as acknowledging their grandeur, he also attempted Ruskin's precise analytical way of describing mountain forms. But unlike Ruskin he knew little about geology, and his accounts are more impressionistic than scientific. Certainly he achieved some vivid descriptive effects:

> There are round one of the heights of the Jungfrau two ends or falls of a glacier. If you took the skin of a white tiger or the deep fell of some other animal and swung it tossing high in the air and then cast it out before you it would fall and so clasp and lap round anything in its way just as this glacier does and the fleece would part in the same rifts: you must suppose a lapis lazuli under-flix to appear. The spraying out of one end I tried to catch but it would have taken hours: it was this which first made me think of a tiger-skin, and it ends in points and tongues like the tail and claws: indeed the ends of the glaciers are knotted or knuckled like talons. Above, in a plane nearly parallel to the eye, becoming thus foreshortened, it forms saddle-curves with dips and swells [J 174].

Ruskin might have found this description a little too fanciful. Here and elsewhere Hopkins follows Ruskin in paying such close attention to detail that one has an imperfect sense of the totality. The attempt to use words with the visual precision of a drawing does, in fact, require completion by something

that presents itself directly to the eye, like the many sketches
with which Ruskin accompanies his minute studies of mountains in Part V of *Modern Painters*. Still, Hopkins's journal of
his Alpine experiences contains some wonderfully vivid descriptive writing, even if one feels closer to the essential note
of his later poetry in a single casual sentence such as "How
fond of and warped to the mountains it would be easy to
become!" Some of the journal entries are of more direct human
interest; noticing a fellow guest in an inn, Hopkins gave a
strongly negative expression of his "fascination with faces":
"there I first saw that repulsive type of French face. It is hard
to seize what it is. The outline is oval but cut away at the
jaws; the eyes are big, shallow-set, close to the eyebrows, and
near, the upper lid straight and long, the lower brought down
to a marked corner in the middle, the pupils large and clear . . ."
and so on, for several more lines of close description that
effectively disintegrates the face into its constituent elements.

On 1st August Hopkins returned to England, after four
weeks of satisfying physical activity and intense visual experience among the mountains. Years later memories of what he had
seen would be transformed into a frightening inner landscape:

> O the mind, mind has mountains; cliffs of fall
> Frightful, sheer, no-man-fathomed.

The next few weeks were spent quietly at home. Visits to the
cathedrals of St. Albans and Ely prompted several pages of
careful architectural description in Hopkins's journal. On 25th
August Bridges, recently back from a tour of the Middle East,
paid a visit and was bitten by Rover, the Hopkins family dog.
The journal entries for early September are brief and matter-
of-fact. They record a round of farewells to friends and family,
including Uncle Charles, now back in England after many years
in Hawaii. On the evening of 7th September Hopkins said
goodbye at home and walked to the local suburban railway
station at Finchley Road. He found he had arrived three-
quarters of an hour too early for his train, so he called on his
Aunt Anne who lived nearby. Anne Hopkins walked back to
the station with the nephew whom she had helped to bring up,

and whose artistic tastes she had done much to foster. He made a second farewell, then travelled by train a few miles across the western fringes of London to Richmond, and on to Roehampton and a new life.

It must have been an emotional occasion for both Hopkins and his family. Within two years the Hopkins parents had had to endure the successive shocks of their son's conversion to Roman Catholicism, his determination to be a priest and finally his entry into the Jesuits, the order whose very name provoked a primitive fear and suspicion in many English people. He was not, it was true, entering a totally enclosed order; he would be living only a few miles away and could remain in touch with family and friends. But the separation was real and must have been painful.

3

The Jesuit

HOPKINS WAS TWENTY-FOUR when he became a Jesuit. His life until then had been materially sheltered and uneventful, though marked by adventures of the intellect and the drama of religious progress. It was, too, a life graced by possibilities, certainly during his years at Balliol, that forcing-house of dominant circles in English society. There was little that an exceptionally gifted pupil of Jowett's might not aspire to, in the Established Church, academic life, the civil service or the law. As an undergraduate Hopkins was in close contact with men who were already, or were to become in time, influential figures in the national culture; as well as Jowett himself there were Pusey and Liddon among religious thinkers, and Pater and Green among secular ones. After his conversion Hopkins would have found fewer opportunities, given the still widespread prejudice against Catholics, though an able and determined Catholic layman could still play an important part in English life, as did Lord Acton in scholarship and the Marquis of Ripon in politics. As a professional man of letters Hopkins might have found a prominent place in the expanding Catholic literary circles of the late nineteenth century, together with such co-religionists as Coventry Patmore and Alice Meynell. But when he became a Jesuit all doors were closed to him. By that decision he moved out of the mainstream of English society into a small, enclosed world that, though it possessed a venerable and rich sub-culture of its own, seemed exotic and even sinister to most Englishmen. T. H. Green wrote with affection of his former pupil after hearing that Hopkins had become a Jesuit, but added:

> I imagine him—perhaps uncharitably—to be one of those, like his ideal J. H. Newman, who instead of simply offering themselves to the revelation of God in the reasonable world, are fain to put themselves in an attitude—saintly, it is true, but still an attitude. . . . It vexes me to the heart to think of a fine nature being victimised by a system which in my "historic conscience" I hold to be subversive of the Family and the State, and which puts the service of an exceptional institution, or the saving of the individual soul, in opposition to the loyal service in society.[1]

Other friends of Hopkins would have shared these sentiments, for the Jesuits were regarded with general suspicion. They were thought of as scheming, prevaricating, disloyal and profoundly un-English in an Italianate or Spanish fashion. It was a suspicion that went back to Elizabethan times. Nevertheless, the English Jesuits were self-confident and expanding rapidly when Hopkins joined the order, and they attracted a steady succession of converts. And however much the Jesuits were regarded as dangerously "foreign" by Victorian Protestant opinion, inside the order there was a strong feeling of English identity. It expressed itself in a sense of community with the Jesuit missionaries and martyrs of Elizabethan times who had died in an attempt to restore the traditional faith of Englishmen, like Edmund Campion, whom Hopkins started to commemorate in a "great ode" in 1881 (though the attempt, like so many of his literary undertakings, came to nothing). The Jesuits' English

[1] Stephen Paget, *Henry Scott Holland: A Memoir* (London: 1921), pp. 29–30.

identity had been not only preserved but given a peculiar strength during the centuries of enforced exile in France and Belgium. For two hundred years the focus of English Jesuit activity had been the house of studies and school at St. Omers, near Calais, which had later to move to Bruges and then to Liège. There was no doubt in the minds of the exiled community that they were English Jesuits and not Frenchmen or Spaniards. Early in the nineteenth century they returned to England, to Stonyhurst in Lancashire, where Hopkins lived and studied from 1870 to 1873.

The Jesuits were not an enclosed monastic order, although they lived the life of a disciplined community. Their work was in the world, in a combination of teaching, study, prayer and contemplation, on lines laid down by their founder St. Ignatius Loyola in the sixteenth century. The preparation for the priesthood, on which Hopkins entered in 1868, was long and arduous. It was—and is—Jesuit practice for priests of the order not to be ordained until the age of thirty-three, the traditional age of Christ at the end of his ministry. The years till then were spent in a pattern of study and teaching rooted in the culture of the Counter-Reformation. The student—known in the order as a "scholastic"—had to be thoroughly trained in classics, mathematics, rhetoric and philosophy, as well as in the various branches of theology. And part of the training was to teach for a time, either in one of the Jesuit schools or in a seminary. But first of all the candidate had to complete a two-year probationary period known as the "novitiate" to test his suitability for the ideals of the order: a modern Jesuit writing on Hopkins has described these as "personal sanctification and the sanctification of one's neighbour."

Hopkins spent his novitiate at Manresa House, Roehampton. This was an elegant neo-classical building dating from the middle of the eighteenth century, formerly known as Bessborough House; when the Jesuits acquired it in 1861 they changed the name to recall the town in Spain where St. Ignatius composed the *Spiritual Exercises*. When Hopkins arrived at Manresa House on 7th September 1868 he was one of a group of six novices, another of whom was, confusingly, also called

Hopkins. For a few days the new novices were kept apart from the rest of the community, whilst they were orientated to their new life; in a brief letter to his mother written at this time Hopkins remarked: "All that occurs to me to say is that we have to keep our rooms tidy to an extraordinary degree." The novices were then plunged into a taxing period of spiritual and institutional initiation known as the Long Retreat. This was a period of thirty days strictly devoted to prayer and meditation according to the system of St. Ignatius, under the guidance of the novice master. A strict silence had to be maintained, apart from three days allowed for recreation, and no letters were sent or received. Once this *rite de passage* was completed, the new entrants were accepted into the community. Each day was given over to a full and repetitive pattern of spiritual and physical activities. After early Mass the novice applied himself to prayer, meditation, spiritual reading, manual work indoors and outdoors, with periods for games and other forms of recreation, all according to a pre-ordained time-table. There was a weekly free day, and in addition to their activities inside the community the novices taught catechism classes to local children.

This way of life provided an effective mode of socializing the novices into the Society of Jesus and its rigorous spiritual goals. Those who found the demands of such a life unacceptable had plenty of time to leave before the two years of the novitiate were over. The full but uneventful pattern of the days left Hopkins little time to write letters and not much to write about when he did. As he remarked to Bridges in a letter of April 1869: "I wd. make this letter longer if I had more to write about. . . ." He was, however, not wholly cut off from his former friends and associates. He received visits from Edward Bond and Alexander Baillie and later in the year from Bridges himself, who was now studying medicine. Already, it seems, Hopkins's combination of a highly-strung temperament and a tendency to poor health had aroused the vigilant concern of his superiors—something that was to happen at intervals throughout the rest of his life—for he noted in a letter to his mother in February that he was not allowed to fast in Lent. Nevertheless, he found other means of self-mortification for as he later noted in his journal, "a penance which I was doing from Jan. 25 to July 25 prevented me from seeing much that half-year." It seems likely that the regular Ignatian exercises in self-examination prescribed for the novices exacerbated Hopkins's habitual tendency to a rather morbid scrupulosity.

He still found time to write journal entries, if only briefly and at long intervals. Soon after arriving at Roehampton he had noted: "Chestnuts as bright as coals or spots of vermilion," anticipating by some years the images of his poem, "Pied Beauty." For the most part his journal entries are of a familiar kind: notes on the weather and the state of nature—on 4th January 1869 he records: "the other evening after a very bright day, the air rinsed quite clear, there was a slash of glowing yolk-coloured sunset"—and on unusual words and forms of speech. By degrees, though, the journal entries become fuller and more personal. Although Hopkins had, as he thought, decisively abandoned poetry, his journal provided him with a means of developing and preserving his poetic apprehensions. He deepens the Ruskinian attitudes of his early diaries and journals, where he is most concerned with the precise, patient delineation of the forms of nature, to express his personal vision of nature as sacramental. This development is apparent in the journal entries for Hopkins's second year at Roehampton. Ruskinian observation is never abandoned; indeed, Hopkins uses it to discover beauty in unexpected places. As one of his prescribed manual tasks Hopkins had on occasion to clean out the urinals, and in February 1870 he noted: "The stone slabs of the urinals even are frosted in graceful sprays." In December of that year, when he had moved to Stonyhurst, he added a further note to this entry: "I have noticed it here also at the seminary: it comes when they have been washed." Hopkins's deepening vision of nature is apparent in a famous entry made in May 1870:

One day when the bluebells were in bloom I wrote the following. I do not think I have ever seen anything more beautiful than the bluebell I have been looking at. I know the beauty of our Lord by it. Its inscape is mixed of strength and grace, like an ash tree [J 199].

The entry goes on in an extended essay in Ruskinian description, but the essence of it lies in the lines just quoted. Hopkins emphasises "beauty" in a way that suggests the aestheticism of the Pre-Raphaelites, but he goes beyond a self-sufficient aestheticism to see natural beauty as a sign of divine beauty, not simply an abstract or transcendental quality but the concrete beauty of Christ. For Hopkins nature manifests Christ, and the Creation and the Incarnation are almost two aspects of a single event. Hopkins developed this conviction by himself but he later found a similar idea of Christ's centrality in the universe in the writings of the medieval philosopher Duns Scotus, whom he first read in 1872 and came to regard with veneration. In his response to the bluebell Hopkins refers to its "inscape." This word, together with "instress," recurs constantly in Hopkins's aesthetic and philosophical reflections. He first used them in his "Notes on Parmenides," written early in 1868, and neither there nor subsequently does he precisely define them. Their sense can, however, be drawn from the multiple contexts in which Hopkins uses them. Later, in 1879, when he had returned to writing poetry, Hopkins told Bridges: "as air, melody, is what strikes me most of all in music and design in painting, so design, pattern or what I am in the habit of calling 'inscape' is what I above all aim at in poetry" (LB 66). "Inscape" was the form or design that was unique to a given entity, whether a poem or a flower, a building or a man, and which distinguished it from all other creation. A recent writer on Hopkins, R. K. R. Thornton, has summed it up succinctly: "If the picture that makes a whole and single thing out of an area of land is a landscape, then what makes up a single thing out of its inner nature would be its 'inscape.' "[2] Hopkins also uses the word as a verb, "to inscape," which, as Mr. Thornton says, "means roughly 'to grasp the pattern of' or sometimes 'to show the pattern of.' " The com-

[2] R. K. R. Thornton, *Gerard Manley Hopkins: The Poems* (London: 1973), p. 19.

panion word "instress" implies "force," both the force that
preserves inscape and enables a thing to cohere in its particular
nature, and that which unites the observer with the object of
his perception: "What you look hard at seems to look hard at
you," Hopkins wrote (J 204). Mr. Thornton provides a concise
summary:

> To put it in a way which does not allow for the subtleties
> and shades of meaning which it acquires for Hopkins, there
> is a force (instress) which makes natural things the way they
> are (shapes their inscape) and there is a power (instress)
> which this shape has to affect the beholder.[3]

The richer implications and shades of meaning of these terms
become apparent as one reads through Hopkins's journal and
letters. Insofar as the idea of "inscape" enabled Hopkins to
think of an object as having its own unique coherence, it val-
uably counter-balanced the disintegratory tendencies of the
Ruskinian mode of minute description.

The two years of the novitiate passed unremarkably, in a
low-key existence designed to train the novice in the theory
and practice of humility and obedience. Though uneventful,
the days were filled by a recurring order of prayer, contemplation, instruction, and manual and domestic work. Hopkins taught the catechism in neighbouring parishes, and learned
to preach, with his fellow-novices as an audience. From December 1869 to February 1870 he served in the rotating post
of porter or chief novice. One of his duties during that time
was to write a journal recording the daily events at Manresa,
which he did with his customary punctilio. It is a functional,
colourless record which contrasts interestingly with the richness of his personal journal. In a letter to his mother in March
1870 Hopkins expressed something of his unique sense of the
world. Enclosing a duck's feather for her birthday, he wrote:

> I practise at present the evangelical poverty which I soon
> hope to vow, but no-one is ever so poor that he is not (with-

[3] Thornton, *op. cit.*, pp. 21–22.

out prejudice to all the rest of the world) owner of the skies
and stars and everything wild that is to be found on the
earth, and out of this immense stock I make over to you my
right to one particular [FL 111].

The novitiate concluded with an eight-day retreat at the end
of August 1870, under the direction of the novice master,
Father Gallway, a priest for whom Hopkins always had a
special affection and who treated him with great kindness in
later years. Then, on 8th September, precisely two years after
arriving at Manresa, Hopkins and three fellow-novices—one
of them his namesake, Frederick Hopkins, later to become
Bishop of British Honduras—took solemn vows of poverty,
chastity and obedience. The ceremony was simple, almost
secret, because at that time the Jesuits were uncertain of their
legal right to function in England. However monotonous the
round of life at Manresa had been, Hopkins was sorry to leave;
indeed he told his mother a few days later that it had come to
seem like a second home. But it was time to move. On 9th
September he wrote in his journal: "To Stonyhurst to the
seminary."

The Jesuit scholastic did not stay in one place for very long.
The successive phases of training were spent in the various
Jesuit houses scattered over England, and Hopkins was sent
to Stonyhurst for the "Philosophate," a three-year period for
the study of philosophy and mathematics. Stonyhurst was the
oldest Jesuit house in England, and was something of a shrine
of the order; it contained books and relics recalling the Elizabethan martyrs and the English Jesuits' two-hundred-year
exile in France and Flanders. Even words commonly used
in ·the community reflected the Jesuits' history. The scholastics' monthly free day was known as a "Blandyke," from
Blandecques, a village near St. Omer where the Jesuits had
once owned a country house, while their annual holiday was
called "Villa," presumably from the Latin for farmhouse.
Stonyhurst lay in a bleak setting on the edge of the Pennines,
more than two hundred miles to the north of London; the surroundings were very different from the pleasant but bland

parkland of Roehampton. But though the moors and hills around Stonyhurst were rugged, they had their own particular beauty, as Hopkins soon acknowledged. Shortly after arriving he wrote to his mother: "The window of the room I am in commands a beautiful range of moors dappled with light and shade." For Hopkins a pied or dappled quality, with contrasting elements held in a larger unity, was of the essence of beauty. The following year, writing to Alexander Baillie, he gave a fuller account of his situation. He complained of the harsh and wet climate, asserting—incorrectly—"we have the highest rain-gauge in England, I believe," but continued:

> nevertheless it is fine scenery, great hills and "fells" with noble outline often, subject to charming effects of light (though I am bound to say that total obscuration is the commonest effect of all), and three beautiful rivers. The clouds in particular are more interesting than in any other place I have seen. But they must be full of soot, for the fleeces of the sheep are quite black with it. We also see the northern lights to advantage at times [FL 234–35].

Hopkins concludes the letter with what he called a "sprig of rhetoric": "this life here though it is hard is God's will for me as I most intimately know, which is more than violets knee-deep."

The journal entries written at Stonyhurst show Hopkins's appreciation of his new surroundings: the hills, the rivers, the spectacular cloud-formations and effects of light so characteristic of the north-west of England. Increasingly he organizes his perceptions with the ideas of "inscape" and "instress," now central to his thinking and constantly acquiring fresh subtlety and richness. And for all his awareness of the larger aspects of nature he could still delight in the small and simple: "Take a *few* primroses in a glass and the instress of—brilliancy, sort of starriness: I have not the right word—so simple a flower gives is remarkable." Sometimes his extreme sensitivity found the facts of change and destruction too much to bear. From his undergraduate days the ash-tree had been one of his favourite forms of nature, and on 8th April 1873 he noted:

The ashtree growing in the corner of the garden was felled. It was lopped first: I heard the sound and looking out and seeing it maimed there came at that moment a great pang and I wished to die and not see the inscapes of the world destroyed any more [J 230].

It was at Stonyhurst that Hopkins began to acquire the reputation he was to bear for the rest of his life among the Jesuits, that of being a gentle eccentric of unpredictable ways. A certain path at Stonyhurst would glitter in the sun after rain, and many years after Hopkins's death an old lay-brother recalled how he would crouch down to peer at it: " 'Ay, a strange young man,' said the old brother, 'crouching down that gate to stare at some wet sand. A fair natural 'e seemed to us, that Mr. 'opkins.' " (J 408). Hopkins's sensitivity was usually balanced by his tough-mindedness and sense of humor; but on occasion, when he was fatigued or in poor health, it became extreme.

Apart from the rigours of the climate and his intermittent fits of depression, Hopkins seems to have quite enjoyed his years at Stonyhurst. There was good country round about for walks and sometimes there was skating in winter. The scholastics took summer holidays in Argyleshire or the Isle of Man, and Hopkins made occasional visits to his family. He spent a week on holiday with them in Hampstead and Hampshire in September 1871, and subsequently told William Garrett that he "found things pleasanter than they have ever been since my conversion, which is a great comfort." He was with them again for Christmas 1872. Immediately afterwards he was operated on—at home—for piles, and spent a fortnight recovering in bed, when he was visited by a succession of Oxford friends: Addis, Wood, Baillie and Bond. Whilst still convalescent Hopkins took the opportunity to indulge his love of painting by visiting the Old Masters exhibition at Burlington House.

Hopkins and his fellow-scholastics did not live in the main building at Stonyhurst, which contained the college, but in the seminary of St. Mary's, a plain barrack-like building some three hundred yards away, which was run as a separate community with its own Superior. In 1870, when Hopkins arrived, the newly-appointed Superior was Father Alfred Weld who, as Provincial, had admitted him into the Society of Jesus two years before. It was the policy of the Jesuits to rotate administrative positions, and to shuffle men about geographically at regular intervals and at short notice, so that paths frequently crossed and re-crossed. Father Weld taught mathematics at St. Mary's, a discipline that Hopkins tolerated but had no great enthusiasm for. As at Roehampton the scholastics' days were divided between individual and liturgical prayer, meditation, study and recreation. But here there was less manual and more intellectual work. The philosophy course was demanding, and not made any easier by being taught entirely in Latin. But for Hopkins, with an Oxford Greats training behind him, it did not present any insuperable difficulties, even though it was in an unfamiliar tradition. The emphasis was heavily on Scholastic philosophy, though the revival of Thomism by Pope Leo XIII was not yet under way, and Aristotle and Aquinas were approached via the seventeenth-century Jesuit commentator Francisco Suarez. Before becoming a Jesuit Hopkins had declared his unqualified admiration for Aristotle—"the end-all and be-all of philosophy"—but at Stonyhurst his enquiring mind led him away from the mainstream of Scholasticism to an intellectual discovery that was to prove of great importance in his aesthetic and intellectual development. In the summer of 1872 he was browsing through the philosophy section of the Stonyhurst library when he came across an early-sixteenth-century work in two volumes called *Scriptum Oxoniense super Sententiis*. This was his first acquaintance with Duns Scotus. On 3rd August Hopkins and his fellow-scholastics went on holiday to the Isle of Man and he wrote in his journal:

At this time I had first begun to get hold of the copy of Scotus on the Sentences in the Baddely library and was flush with a new stroke of enthusiasm. It may come to

nothing or it may be a mercy from God. But just then when
I took in any inscape of the sky or sea I thought of Scotus
[J 221].

Scotus was a Franciscan philosopher of the early fourteenth
century, born in Scotland or northern England, who originated
a minority tradition in Scholastic thought, different from the
dominant one of Aquinas. Scotus was known as the "Subtle
Doctor" and his ideas are not easy to unravel, even for those
trained in Scholastic philosophy. An explanation of Scotist
thought is far beyond the scope of the present study or the
competence of its author. What is important is the appeal of
certain ideas of Scotus for Hopkins, primarily, it seems, because they gave a venerable philosophical authentication to
some of his own insights. Scotus made much of the distinction
between general nature and the particular, unique individuality
of a person or thing. This uniqueness he expressed in the word
haeccitas, or "thisness," which seemed to Hopkins to corre-
spond to his own word "inscape." Again, there was Scotus's
emphasis on the Incarnation of Christ as lying at the heart of
creation, and his devotion to the Blessed Virgin. Hopkins took
from Scotus what he needed, and henceforth had a particular
affection for the Franciscan which he later expressed in his
sonnet, "Duns Scotus's Oxford": "who of all men most sways
my spirits to peace." Hopkins's predilection for Scotism rather
than the dominant Thomist Scholastic tradition deepened his
reputation for eccentricity and may even have attracted sus-
picions of doctrinal heterodoxy.

At Stonyhurst Hopkins lived in a small, geographically isolated community, dedicated to the cultivation of spiritual and
intellectual life. But there was a world elsewhere, which could
not be altogether ignored. It made its presence felt in the
sooty fleece of the sheep on the moors around Stonyhurst,
blackened by smoke from the Lancashire industrial towns a
few miles away. On occasional visits to these towns the
scholastics saw something of the poverty of the people. Hopkins was a keen reader of newspapers whenever he could get
hold of them, and his quick, probing intelligence directed itself

to politics as well as philosophy. His reflections on the state of society produced the so-called "red letter" which he wrote to Bridges on 2nd August 1871. It is a remarkable contribution to the contemporary debate on the Condition of England engaged in by Carlyle and Ruskin and other Victorian thinkers:

> I am afraid some great revolution is not far off. Horrible to say, in a manner I am a Communist. Their ideal bating some things is nobler than that professed by any secular statesman I know of (I must own I live in bat-light and shoot at a venture). Besides it is just—I do not mean the means of getting to it are. But it is a dreadful thing for the greatest and most necessary part of a very rich nation to live a hard life without dignity, knowledge, comforts, delights, or hopes in the midst of plenty—which plenty they make. They profess that they do not care what they wreck and burn, the old civilization and order must be destroyed. This is a dreadful look out but what has the old civilization done for them? As it at present stands in England it is itself in great measure founded on wrecking. But they get none of the spoils, they came in for nothing but harm from it then and thereafter. England has grown hugely wealthy but this wealth has not reached the working classes; I expect it has made their condition worse. Besides this iniquitous order the old civilization embodies another order mostly old and what is new in direct entail from the old, the old religion, learning, law, art, etc and all the history that is preserved in standing monuments. But as the working classes have not been educated they know next to nothing of all this and cannot be expected to care if they destroy it. The more I look the more black and deservedly black the future looks, so I will write no more [LB 27–28].

Although Hopkins wrote that "In a manner I am a Communist," his critique was that of a Tory radical rather than a socialist: he wanted the working class to be given their rightful place in the existing social order rather than see that order overthrown, as he explained near the end of his life in a commentary on his poem, "Tom's Garland." This letter was written against the

background of violent events in France in 1871, following the
Franco-Prussian War: the establishment of the Commune in
Paris and the murder of the Archbishop of Paris and other
hostages by the Communards—as noted by Hopkins in his
journal in May—followed by the bloody suppression of the
Commune. A few days after writing to Bridges Hopkins wrote
in his journal: "The Battle of Dorking and the fear of the
Revolution make me sad now," referring to a best-selling popular novel of the time which described the invasion and defeat
of England by a Prussian army. Bridges, a young man of strong
and conventionally Tory opinions, seems to have been out-
raged by this letter—at least, he did not reply and the correspondence was broken off until early in 1874, when Hopkins
wrote: "if this was your reason for not answering it seems to
shew a greater keenness about politics than is common."

Hopkins kept up as well as he could with recent books. In
March 1873 he includes in a letter to his mother a delightful
paragraph in praise of Edward Lear's "new Book of Nonsense,"
which suggests something of Hopkins's very Victorian sense
of humour and love of absurdity and word-play. Later in the
year he tells Edward Bond that he is reading Matthew Arnold's
poems "with more interest than rapture, as you will easily
understand, for they seem to have all the ingredients of poetry
without quite being it," and has just read Newman's *Grammar
of Assent*, published three years earlier. Hopkins gives only
very qualified approval to Newman's philosophical treatise,
finding in it "a narrow circle of instance and quotation" and
"a real want of brilliancy," though he acknowledges Newman
as "our greatest living master of style." But the *Grammar of
Assent* must have impressed Hopkins more deeply than he
indicates here, for in 1883 he proposed to Newman that he
write a commentary on it, a proposal which Newman graciously
declined.

In June 1873 Hopkins concluded the Philosophate with an
examination. That phase of his training was now over and he
anticipated that he would next be required to teach in a Jesuit
school for a time, perhaps in the college at Stonyhurst. Indeed,
he writes to his mother from the Isle of Man, where he is on

holiday, that he will shortly begin teaching for a year. He adds: "The year's teaching was given as a rest. I think this is as good an arrangement as could have been made." As always, Hopkins's superiors needed to keep an eye on his health and nervous condition; the previous Lent he had again been excused from fasting, and his work was lightened. He was on the Isle of Man for a fortnight, during which time he climbed to the highest point of the island, Snae Fell, from which one could see England, Scotland and Ireland. He made a characteristic observation in his journal: "The day was bright; pied skies. On the way back we saw eight or perhaps ten hawks together." Other journal entries contain vivid descriptions of the appearance and behaviour of the sea. Soon after the seminarians returned to Stonyhurst they gave a concert, as described by an entry in the "Beadle's Log":

> August 21. Thursday. As usual except that the Seminarians gave an entertainment after supper. . . . It consisted of music, comic and half-comic pieces etc. It was mainly got up by Mr. G. Hopkins, and was a decided success.[4]

It is pleasant to be reminded that Hopkins, for all his sensitivity and tendency to depression, was capable of such genial activities. Then, on 27th August, he finally received news of his next assignment. He was not, after all, to remain at Stonyhurst but was to return to Roehampton, for which he left the very next morning. A milder climate had been thought appropriate.

As soon as Hopkins arrived at Manresa he went into a nine-day retreat, during which he received what he cryptically called "a great mercy about Dolben." When it was over he met his students, a group of "Juniors," that is to say, scholastics who had just emerged from the novitiate and were beginning the study of "Rhetoric." Hopkins acquired the grandiose title of "Professor of Rhetoric," and his duties involved the teaching of Latin, Greek, English and some French. The work was, in principle, by no means hard for someone as qualified as Hop-

---

[4] Alfred Thomas, *Hopkins the Jesuit* (London: 1969), p. 127.

kins; certainly the scholastics, so well trained in humility and obedience, were easier to teach than schoolboys. There is no reason to doubt that the Jesuits intended Hopkins to have a fairly easy year, and in some respects he did. He had a good deal of free time and often went to London to look at pictures. Soon after arriving at Roehampton, on 18th September, which was a Blandyke or free day, he visited the Kensington Museum, now the Victoria and Albert Museum. He spent Christmas with his family and during the holiday went with his brother Arthur to an exhibition of water colours. Later journal entries record visits to the Sloane Museum, the National Gallery and, again, the Kensington Museum. In May and June 1874 Hopkins twice visited that year's Royal Academy and wrote several pages of notes on what he saw there, including paintings by Millais, Alma Tadema, Leighton and Tissot. He also noted a fashionable innovation in taste: "Bright Japanese pictures are the rage." After his second visit to the Academy Hopkins went on to the church of All Saints in Margaret Street, in order to see whether he still preserved his old enthusiasm for the work of its architect, William Butterfield, and found that, with some reservations, he did. Other expeditions during the year included visits to both Houses of Parliament and a day spent in the law courts listening to the Lord Chief Justice summing up at the end of the Tichbourne Case. This celebrated and intricate legal battle greatly interested Hopkins during the several years it dragged on. It concerned the long lost heir of the Tichbourne name and baronetcy, Roger Tichbourne, and the so-called claimant, Arthur Orton, a butcher's son from Wapping, who alleged that he was in fact the heir who had disappeared in 1854. Roger Tichbourne had been educated at Stonyhurst for three years, hence Hopkins's particular interest. There was much discussion of the accuracy of the claimant's supposed recollections of life there. Orton was finally sentenced to fourteen years' imprisonment for perjury. These outings gave Hopkins a renewed taste for London, which he looked back to nostalgically during his later years, particularly during his exile in Dublin. But nature was, as always, Hopkin's primary love, and there are some vivid descriptions in his journals at this time, where he is able to transcend Ruskinian minuteness and present an impression as a precise totality. One instance occurs in a note at the end of October 1873:

> At the end of the month hard frosts. Wonderful downpour of leaf: when the morning sun began to melt the frost they fall at one touch and in a few minutes a whole tree was flung of them; they lay masking and papering the ground at the foot. Then the tree seems to be looking down on its cast self as blue sky on snow after a long fall, its losing, its doing [J 239].

Reading such passages, one realises that Hopkins was again, or had never ceased to be, a poet, even though his journal entries lack what he would have regarded as the necessary form of poetry. But this observation clearly looks forward to such a poem as "Spring and Fall." In a very different way another journal entry anticipates the poetry of Hopkins's later years. In September he suffered from an appalling nightmare, which he described with startling precision over a long paragraph. Hopkins summed up the sensation: "The feeling is terrible: the body no longer swayed as a piece by the muscular and nervous instress seems to fall in and hang like a dead weight on the chest. I cried on the holy name and by degrees recovered myself as I thought to do" (J 238). Some similar disturbing experience, though translated from physical into spiritual terms, seems to have prompted the "terrible sonnets" of the Dublin years.

The most tangible record of Hopkins's year of teaching at Roehampton lies in the lecture notes headed "Rhythm and the Other Structural Parts of Rhetoric." The notes are very thorough and carefully ordered; they reflect all of Hopkins's subtlety of mind, and suggest that the lectures made considerable demands on the listeners. The notes are mostly concerned with problems of rhythm, metre and prosody, primarily in Latin and Greek, but also in passages taken from English and French and other modern languages. Not all of these questions are likely to be of great interest, or even fully intelligible, to the modern student of vernacular literature. But there are places in the notes where Hopkins reflects on more general literary matters and reveals himself a critic and theorist of great insight. This is so, for instance, in his comments on rhyme, and above all in the separate note headed "Poetry and Verse," where he sets out some fundamental considerations:

> Poetry is speech framed for contemplation of the mind by the way of hearing or speech framed to be heard for its own sake and interest even over and above its interest of meaning. Some matter and meaning is essential to it but only as an element necessary to support and employ the shape which is contemplated for its own sake [J 289].

Such a passage provides a direct link between the Scholastic view of art as that which pleases on being seen, and the Symbolist and Modernist poetics of our own age. The notes also have an oblique relevance to Hopkins's own later poetry. Their prosodic speculations provided the matrix for his later rationalization of his own metrical innovations as "sprung rhythm."

This period at Roehampton should have provided Hopkins with the rest, or at least the stimulating change, that his superiors had intended for him. His duties were not onerous, the work was intellectually absorbing and the cultural satisfactions of London were at hand. Nevertheless, by the end of his time there he was consumed by fatigue and depression:

> Our schools at Roehampton ended with two days of examination before St. Ignatius' feast the 31st. I was very tired and seemed deeply cast down till I had some kind words from the Provincial. Altogether perhaps my heart has never been so burdened and cast down as this year. The tax on my strength has been greater than I have felt before: at least now at Teignmouth I feel myself weak and can do little. But in all this our Lord goes His own way [J 249–50].

In the past Hopkins had expressed similar complaints about being discouraged and fatigued, notably during his period as a teacher at the Oratory School, and was to again in the future as a professor in Dublin. Writing to Bridges the following year, he says he wished he could have seen him while at Roehampton: "what a pleasure it would have been and what a break in the routine of rhetoric, which I taught so badly and so painfully." It is hard to avoid the conclusion that Hopkins's sensitivity and intellectual scrupulousness unfitted him for the role of teacher, even though that was what he was destined to be for much of his later life. When he wrote this note he was on holiday at Teignmouth in Devon, and before long his spirits lifted, as they usually did when he was on vacation, and he devoted several pages of his journal to characteristic descriptions of the Devon countryside and the architecture of the local churches. An entry for 17th August reveals a positive exaltation of spirit as well as anticipating a poem, "The Starlight Night": "As we drove home the stars came out thick: I leant back to look at them and my heart opening more than usual praised our Lord to and in whom all that beauty comes home." Without being reductively clinical about Hopkins, such intense alternations of feeling might nowadays be regarded as manic-depressive.

Sometimes Jesuit scholastics had to spend several years as teachers, but in Hopkins's case one year was considered sufficient. Back in Roehampton after his holiday, he heard on 26th August 1874 that he was to move to the Jesuit house of St. Beuno's in North Wales for the next and final phase of his training, the "Theologate." The notice was, as always, very brief and two days later Hopkins was there. St. Beuno's had been established in the 1840s by Father Randall Lythgoe, one of the pioneers in the Jesuit revival in England, and was deliberately chosen for its seclusion and natural beauty. The day after Hopkins arrived he gave his father some account of his situation:

The house stands on a steep hillside, it commands the long-drawn valley of the Clwyd to the sea, a vast prospect, and opposite is Snowdon and its range, just now it being bright visible but coming and going with the weather. The air seems to me very fresh and wholesome. Holidays till the 2nd of

October. After that hours of study very close—lectures in dogmatic theology, moral ditto, canon law, church history, scripture, Hebrew and what not. I have half a mind to get up a little Welsh: all the neighbours speak it [FL 124].

Life at St. Beuno's, a rambling neo-Gothic building, had its physical hardships: there were frequent complaints about the inadequacies of the very primitive central heating, and some of the bedrooms were uninhabitable in winter. Nevertheless, it was there,

> Away in the lovable west,
> On a pastoral forehead of Wales,

that Hopkins spent the happiest years of his adult life and where he returned to the practice of poetry.

The casual reference to learning Welsh is significant. Hopkins was always passionately interested in language, and in his journal he often lists uncommon or dialect words and engages in philological speculation. His interest in Welsh had been first aroused ten years before when he had copied an inscription in that language into his undergraduate notebooks. Within a day or so he had begun to study Welsh, though not without a crisis of conscience. Writing in his journal in September, Hopkins says that he has begun learning Welsh but is worried about the purity of his intentions. He consulted the Rector of St. Beuno's, Father Jones, who said, with Jesuit practicality, that the only proper reason for learning Welsh was to help in the conversion of the local people. Hopkins pondered this question with all the agonized scrupulosity of which he was capable; it seemed to him that part of his motive was, indeed, to work for the conversion of the Welsh but not, perhaps, a sufficient part. He sadly decided that he would have to give up Welsh, but this was evidently not his final decision, whatever Father Jones had recommended, because in fact he continued to study the language and took lessons from a local lady called Miss Jones. By the middle of 1876 he was very interested in the metrical patterns of Welsh poetry and had become proficient enough to write some poems in the language. Meantime he was also finding out something about Maltese from a Maltese scholastic called Brother Magri.

In September 1874 Hopkins received the minor clerical orders, as a step towards his final ordination as a priest. He wrote to his mother: "I received the tonsure and the four minor orders yesterday. The tonsure consisted of five little snips but the bishop must have found even that a hard job, for I had cut my hair to the scalp, as it happened, just before." Then followed a heavy three-year programme of theological study. Hopkins found moral theology, of the technical, legalistic kind then prevalent in the Catholic Church, particularly exacting. Being so much given to anxiety when assessing his own motives and conduct, he took this branch of study, intended to qualify the priest to hear confessions, with immense seriousness. He told his mother it was "the most wearisome work." But the surrounding country, the prospect of the mountains and the sea in the distance, provided refreshment of spirit. Hopkins's manuscript journal breaks off abruptly in the middle of an entry for 7th February 1875, whilst he is recording an item of local folklore. The last few pages record many walks round about St. Beuno's, with notes on skies and sunsets, as well as visits to places further afield like Denbigh and the miraculous spring at Holywell of St. Winefride, niece of St. Beuno. The spring, Hopkins later wrote, "fills me with devotion every time I see it."

Hopkins also found time to revive his correspondence with Bridges, which had virtually lapsed since the "red letter" of 1871. Hopkins's letters suggest that there was still an element of constraint, almost of asperity, between them. Bridges objected to the Jesuit rule that all incoming letters had to be censored, though Hopkins assured him that this was no more than a formality. Despite his personal affection for Hopkins, Bridges made no secret of his disapproval of Catholicism in general and the Jesuits in particular. Stung by a disparaging comment, Hopkins on one occasion remarked: "You say you don't like Jesuits. Did you ever see one?" But the discussion of poetry still provided common ground even if, there, too, disagreements were frequent. Bridges, who was extremely

reticent about his own poetry, had published a volume of poems
in 1873, a fact unknown to Hopkins until he chanced to read
a review of it in the *Academy*. Until then he had had no idea
that his friend was a poet at all, and he expressed his surprise
and pleasure when he wrote to Bridges early in 1874. There
followed another long delay until 1877, when Bridges sent
him two pamphlets, containing his sonnet sequence, *The
Growth of Love*, and a Latin poem on the history of St.
Bartholomew's Hospital, where Bridges was working as a
physician. In his long reply dated 3rd April 1877 Hopkins is,
first, both appreciative and dismissive of the Latin poem: "I
don't know when I remember to have read so much good Latin
verse together, still I look upon such a performance as a waste
of time and money (a pretty penny it must have cost you
printing)" (LB 33). Hopkins takes the sonnets much more
seriously and comments on them at length. He is very admiring—the sonnets are "truly beautiful"—but he is critical about
many points of detail. This letter is the first of many in which
Hopkins engaged in close, patient, critical comment on his
friends' poems; Bridges was to receive many more, and so in
later years were Richard Watson Dixon and Coventry Patmore.
After discussing *The Growth of Love* Hopkins goes on to
more general remarks about poetry. He says that he has become very interested in Milton, and that he has himself been
experimenting with the sonnet form. He says he will send
recent examples of his work to Bridges: "You will see that my
rhythms go further than yours do in the way of irregularity."
That was an understatement. Hopkins's sonnets—probably
"God's Grandeur" and "The Starlight Night"—were in every
way unlike Bridge's immaculate Parnassianism. It was a casual
enough way of letting his friend know that, after many years
of silence, Hopkins was himself writing poetry again.

He returned to poetry in December 1875. It was a month of
severe weather and on the 7th a German steamship, the
Deutschland, taking emigrants from Bremen to Canada, ran
aground in a snowstorm and was wrecked on a shoal in the
Thames estuary. The ship took more than twenty-four hours
to break up and sink, whilst a storm raged. There were no

attempts at rescue and the passengers and crew suffered ap-
pallingly until the survivors were finally taken off the next
morning. Over sixty people were drowned, among them five
Franciscan nuns who had been exiled from Germany by a
law against religious orders and were sailing to a new life in
Canada. There were full and harrowing reports of the wreck,
first in *The Times* and then in the *Illustrated London News*,
the latter accompanied by drawings. Hopkins was, as he told
his mother, much affected by these accounts and asked her to
send him further cuttings. "I am writing something on this
wreck," he added. When he told the Rector of St. Beuno's
about the deep impression the disaster had made upon him,
Father Jones expressed the wish that someone would commemorate it in a poem. Hopkins interpreted this as a hint that
he should attempt to write one himself and that his resolution
to give up poetry, "unless it were by the wish of my superiors,"
need no longer bind him. He had written no verse since 1868
apart from what he called "two or three little presentation
pieces," one of them a set of Greek iambics to commemorate
the visit of Bishop Vaughan of Salford to Stonyhurst in 1872.
"My hand was out at first," he told Canon Dixon, but before long he was engrossed in writing "The Wreck of the
Deutschland." He began with a deceptively direct account of
the ship setting sail:

> On Saturday sailed from Bremen,
>   American-outward-bound,
> Take settler and seamen, tell men with women
>   Two hundred souls in the round.

But the poem became more elaborate in the course of composition, for Hopkins found himself concerned with much more
than a shipwreck, and this stanza was placed in the middle of
the poem. The first part is certainly an account of some pro-
found religious experience of his own, even though Christopher
Devlin may have claimed too much in confidently locating
this experience in the first week of the Long Retreat during
Hopkins's noviceship, seven years before. But the influence
of Ignatian techniques of meditation is clear enough, with

successive stages of the experience being brought vividly before the senses. In its later section the poem moves on from the shipwreck to a consideration of the spiritual state of England, a matter of perennial concern to Hopkins. And the whole poem is an exercise in experimental metrics: "I had long had haunting my ear the echo of a new rhythm which now I realised on paper." The form of the poem was based on the Pindaric ode, combining a complicated stanzaic pattern with a loose, rhapsodic and digressive development. Ten years of suppressed feeling burst forth in this poem, which has nothing in common with the careful, conventionally devout poetry that Hopkins wrote at Oxford. Yet in writing "The Wreck of the *Deutschland*" Hopkins may have been recalling one of his early poems, "Heaven-Haven." There a nun desires to go "To fields where flies no sharp and sided hail":

> Where no storms come,
> Where the green swell is in the havens dumb,
> And out of the swing of the sea.

In the later poem these desires are negated: the sea is overwhelming and destructive, and the snow-storm is bitter. Yet "The Wreck of the *Deutschland*" also contains a nun; this time the striking figure of the tall German nun calling on Christ *in extremis*, vividly described in newspaper reports. And in the last stanza of "The Wreck of the *Deutschland*" Hopkins repeats the phrase, "heaven-haven." The two poems have similar but antithetical images; the difference between them is the difference between two concepts of the spiritual life: a superficial calm and assurance set against the necessity of struggle and endurance. The relevance to Hopkins's own religious development is evident.

"The Wreck of the *Deutschland*" is now among the most famous poems in the English language. It is also, as much as it was a hundred years ago, one of the strangest and most difficult, "the dragon folded in the gate" of Hopkins's poetry, as Bridges called it. In our own time the difficulty has called forth any number of would-be dragon-slayers in the form of commentators and explicators. We do not know what the

Rector of St. Beuno's made of the poem when he came to read it, but it can hardly have been what he expected. We do, however, have the testimony of one of Hopkins's fellow-scholastics, Father Clement Barraud: "I heard the bard himself read parts of 'The Wreck of the *Deutschland*,' which he was writing at the time, and could hardly understand one line of it."[5] At first Hopkins thought the poem was going to be published in the Jesuits' magazine, *The Month*. He told his mother in a letter of 26th June 1876 that he had written to the editor, Father Henry Coleridge, whom he thought of as his oldest friend in the Society, asking if he would publish it, though adding with typical scrupulosity: "I felt sure he wd. personally dislike it very much, only that he was to consider not his tastes but those of the *Month*'s readers." Father Coleridge knew something of Hopkins's literary talents and was accustomed to printing devotional poetry; a few years before *The Month* had published Newman's *Dream of Gerontius*. His initial reply, before Hopkins sent him the poem, was encouraging. "He replied that there was in America a new sort of poetry which did not rhyme or scan or construe [presumably Father Coleridge was referring to Whitman]; if mine rhymed and scanned and construed, and did not make nonsense or bad morality he did not see why it shd. not do" (FL 138). Hopkins sent him the poem and after some delays was told it would appear in the August number of *The Month*, provided Hopkins removed the accents which marked the scanning. Hopkins was reluctant to do this, but told his mother: "Still I am afraid I must humour an editor, but some lines at all events will have to be marked." The poem did not, however, appear in the August number, and writing to his father on 6th August, Hopkins said: "Tell my mother that my poem is not in the August *Month* and whether it will be in the September number or in any I cannot find out: altogether it has cost me a good deal of trouble." Sometime in the next few weeks Hopkins heard that "The Wreck of the *Deutschland*" would not, after all, be appearing in *The Month*.

[5] "C.B.," "Recollections of Fr. Gerard Hopkins," *The Month*, July 1919.

It must have been a severe disappointment, for he evidently had high hopes for the poem, but he took the blow with calm resignation and at the end of September wrote: "About the *Deutschland* 'sigh no more,' I am glad now it has not appeared."

In a letter to Canon Dixon in 1878 Hopkins referred to the fate of the poem:

> I had to mark the stresses in blue chalk, and this and my rhymes carried on from one line into another and certain chimes suggested by the Welsh poetry I had been reading (what they call *cynghanedd*) and a great many more oddnesses could not but dismay an editor's eye, so that when I offered it to our magazine the *Month*, though at first they accepted it, after a time they withdrew and dared not print it [LD 15].

It looks as if Father Coleridge, though not the first editor to change his mind about a contribution he could not understand, acted very inconsiderately. There is some account of the situation in a reported conversation with Father Smith, then a fellow-scholastic of Hopkins's at St. Beuno's:

> The editor at that time was Fr. Henry Coleridge, a convert clergyman and a scholar of the old-fashioned classical type. He read the poem and could not understand it, and he did not relish publishing any poem that he himself could not master. He then handed the poem to Sydney Smith who did his best to master the author's elaborate system of diacritical signs. But it was not of any service to him. He told me that the short line (Stanza 30, line 4) "Thou hadst glory of this nun?" was one that he read and read again, without being sure that he was reading it with the exact rhythm desired by G.M.H. In the end, as he said to me, "the only result was to give me a very bad headache, and to lead me to hand the poem back to Father Coleridge with the remark that it was indeed unreadable . . ." [J 382].

An ironic footnote to this conversation is that in later years Father Smith became well known for his lack of interest in literature; when he himself became editor of *The Month* he declined to publish any poetry at all.

It is not surprising that Father Coleridge did not understand "The Wreck of the *Deutschland*," since no-one else did at the time. Although Hopkins's metrical experiments and innovations derived from his classical training, they were bound to seem outlandish to readers with a similar background but a more conventional cast of mind. What is inexplicable, though, is that Father Coleridge should in the first place have accepted the poem. My own guess is that he felt a great deal of personal good will towards Hopkins and wanted to print his poem if at all possible, and that when he wrote to Hopkins in June saying it would appear in the August issue he had still not read it properly, though he had seen enough to be struck by Hopkins's system of diacritical markings. When he did read the poem carefully he was dismayed, a reaction which was reinforced by his conversation with Father Smith. The diacritical markings may well have become a point of contention. Hopkins thought them essential as a guide to the reader, and as he said in his letter to his mother of 26th June, he was not at all happy about removing them. Although he wanted the poem published he was obstinate enough to refuse to make many concessions on this point, and his refusal may have given Father Coleridge the excuse he needed not to publish it. It is significant that in his letter to Canon Dixon Hopkins refers to the stress marks as the first of the "oddnesses" that "could not but dismay an editor's eye." When Hopkins says, in his letter to his father of 6th August: "altogether it has cost me a good deal of trouble," he could be referring to recent correspondence with Father Coleridge about these modifications.

This was not quite the end of Hopkins's attempts to appear in *The Month*. In 1878 he tried again with "The Loss of the *Eurydice*" and met a firm rejection. Thereafter he gave up trying to publish his poems, though he did not object to the idea of posthumous publication, if that were God's will. It is tempting but idle to speculate on what might have happened if Father Coleridge had, after all, published "The Wreck of the *Deutschland*." If one poem were published, others would have followed, and it is conceivable that Hopkins's genius would have been quickly recognised and that his example might have changed the course of English poetry in the last quarter of the nineteenth century. But it is more likely that he would have been regarded as an oddity, with few readers and no noticeable influence. Bridges was immensely cautious in waiting so long to publish Hopkins's poems, but his timing seems to have been essentially right; even so, Hopkins's achievement was not finally recognized until the 1930s, more than forty years after his death.

Bridges was at first quite unappreciative of "The Wreck of the *Deutschland*" when Hopkins sent him the manuscript after they had resumed their correspondence in 1877. We do not know precisely what he said but the temper of his remarks can be gauged from Hopkins's sharp but resigned riposte:

> You say you wd. not for any money read my poem again. Nevertheless I beg you will. Besides money, you know, there is love. If it is obscure do not bother yourself with the meaning but pay attention to the best and most intelligible stanzas, as the two last of each part and the narrative of the wreck. If you had done this you wd. have liked it better and sent me some serviceable criticisms, but now your criticism is no use, being only a protest memorializing me against my whole policy and proceedings [LB 46–47].

Bridges's lack of appreciation must have been as great a disappointment to Hopkins as the rejection by *The Month*. And he did not get any more real understanding from the two other poets with whom he corresponded in later years. Canon Dixon always expressed a warm general admiration for Hopkins's poetry but had evident reservations about "The Wreck of the *Deutschland*." He told Hopkins in 1880: "The Deutschland is enormously powerful: it has however such elements of deep distress in it that one reads it with less excited delight though not with less interest than the others." Four years later Coventry Patmore was cool about Hopkins's poems in general and "The Wreck" in particular: "I do not think that I could ever become sufficiently accustomed to your favourite Poem,

'The Wreck of the Deutschland,' to reconcile me to its strangenesses."

Hopkins never wrote anything else as long, as elaborate and as packed with what he himself called "oddnesses." Yet once it was written, he regarded himself as no longer bound by his vow to abstain from writing verse unless under orders, and other, more conventional poems followed before long. Among these was "The Silver Jubilee," commemorating the twenty-fifth anniversary of Dr. James Brown, Bishop of Shrewsbury, in which diocese St. Beuno's was included (it was also the twenty-fifth anniversary of the re-establishment of the Catholic hierarchy). Dr. Brown visited the college in July 1876 on the occasion of the anniversary, and to commemorate it the Jesuits presented him with an album containing a prose address and verse compositions in many languages, drawing on the linguistic skills of the community. Hopkins told his father with a certain note of pride: "For the Welsh they had to come to me, for, sad to say, no one else in the house knows anything about it; I also wrote in Latin and English . . ." (FL 140). The English poem, "The Silver Jubilee," is a slight but graceful set of quatrains, totally unlike "The Wreck of the *Deutschland*." The Welsh poem Hopkins wrote on this occasion is something of a curiosity. It is called "Cywydd," this being the name of the verse form and not a title. In the opinion of modern scholars the Welsh is very faulty and the use of *cynghanedd* is incorrect throughout. Hopkins no doubt regarded the poem purely as an exercise, akin to the Greek and Latin verses he had been accustomed to composing since boyhood; another piece of surviving Welsh verse, a translation of a Latin hymn attributed to St. Francis Xavier, is less ambitious and more correct. Whatever doubts and scruples he had felt at first, Hopkins had persisted in studying Welsh, even though he was over-reaching himself in trying to write poetry in a language of which he had only an imperfect comprehension. Several months later he told Alexander Baillie that although he could read easy prose in Welsh and speak it stumblingly, he still could not understand the spoken language properly and could make very little of the poetry. Father Gallway, who had succeeded Father

Jones as Rector, seems to have taken a positive view of these Welsh studies, for in the spring of 1877 Hopkins spent some days with the Welsh-speaking parish priest of Caernarvon specifically to help his Welsh.

Another piece of pleasant occasional verse was "Penmaen Pool," which Hopkins wrote for the visitors' book of an inn which he visited when on holiday in Merionethshire in August. It was not, however, until the following year, 1877, that he really emerged as a poet and showed conclusively that "The Wreck of the *Deutschland*" was not an isolated outburst. It was indeed something of an *annus mirabilis* for him; within a few months he wrote some of his best-loved poems, such as "God's Grandeur," "The Starlight Night," "Spring," "The Windhover," "Pied Beauty," "Hurrahing in Harvest" and "The Lantern Out of Doors," among others. Mostly in sonnet form, they are fervent expressions of joy in the beauty of nature and a world "charged with the grandeur of God." They express in a more formal and concentrated way the insights that Hopkins had long been recording in his journal, and are pure and memorable statements of his sacramental vision. They also remind one, in a directly autobiographical way, of Hopkins's happiness during his years in North Wales, despite the pressure of his studies.

Hopkins's time at St. Beuno's was coming to an end. Throughout 1877 he was preparing for ordination to the priesthood. As we have seen, he found the course in moral theology a fatiguing and wearisome business, though in March 1877 he was successfully examined and found competent to hear confessions. Then followed one of those slightly farcical misadventures that occurred at intervals in Hopkins's practical life. On 11th March he preached a practice sermon, known as a "Dominical," to his fellow theologians. It was on a text from St. John's Gospel, "Make the men sit down," referring to the miracle of the loaves and fishes. On the page this seems an admirable sermon, both in a literary and a devotional sense. Hopkins begins in the approved Ignatian manner by inviting his listeners to contemplate the scriptural episode, dwelling on the time, place and occasion. He compares the setting of the

Sea of Galilee with the Clwyd Valley, pointing out topo-graphical parallels. The sermon proceeds with elaboration and subtlety, drawing as much as possible out of the initial text, in a traditionally rhetorical way. Still it bears something of Hopkins's familiar cast of mind in its unexpected blend of the homely and the elevated, and in one personal passage he speaks with striking self-knowledge:

> If we are sad we think we shall never be happy more, though the same thing has happened to us times and times; if we are sick we despair of ever being well, though human nature every day is in some one or other sickening and recovering; if in poverty we despair of ever being better off, though the times keep turning and changing; if tired we complain as if no sleep or rest would ever refresh us; if the winter is cold we make believe it will never be summer again. I speak of what I know in myself, and it may be something of the same is true in you [SD 230].

Yet something went fatally wrong when the sermon was de-livered. It may have been too elaborate and literary for its listeners, or it may be that Hopkins's manner prevented them from taking it seriously. He left a wry note at the end of the manuscript:

> This was a Dominical and was delivered on Mid-Lent Sunday March 11 1877 as far as the blue pencilmark on the sheet before this. People laughed at it prodigiously, I saw some of them roll on their chairs with laughter. This made me lose the thread, so that I did not deliver the last two paragraphs right but mixed things up. The last paragraph, in which *Make the men sit down* is often repeated, far from having a good effect, made them roll more than ever [SD 233].

In July Hopkins took his final examinations in theology, then spent three weeks with his family in Hampstead, during which time he visited Bridges. He had expected to spend a further year at St. Beuno's, continuing his studies after ordina-tion. But his superiors had other plans for him, to his con-siderable disappointment. In August he returned to St. Beuno's to spend his last few weeks there. Then, in September, preparations for ordination began. First, there was a retreat beginning on the 15th. Then, on 21st and 22nd September, Hopkins received the major orders of subdeacon and deacon, respectively. Finally, on Sunday 23rd September, Hopkins and fifteen others were raised to the priesthood by Bishop Brown. It was a day of festivity, with guests and a special lunch, concluding with an impromptu concert, a solemn *Te Deum* and Benediction. Hopkins had waited nine years for this great day, since entering the Jesuit novitiate in September 1868, but he makes no reference to it in his surviving correspondence.

He was now ready to leave St. Beuno's, but before he could do so a bout of illness intervened, necessitating another minor but disagreeable operation. This time he had to be circumcised. After a few days in bed Hopkins made a good recovery, and on 19th October he left to take up his next assignment, at Mount St. Mary's College, near Sheffield.

4

The Two Vocations

AFTER THE THREE stable and generally happy years at St.
Beuno's the newly ordained Father Hopkins passed to an
unsettled mode of life. It was a basic principle of the Society
of Jesus that the Jesuit must always be ready to move at a
moment's notice wherever his superiors thought he could be
most useful. Even so, Hopkins was subjected to a remarkable
number of moves in the first few years of his priesthood. The
problem for the Jesuits was in knowing what to do with him.
He was regarded in the order as a man of intellectual brilliance
and high academic attainments, with a likeable but highly-
strung personality. His health was not robust and he had a
reputation for eccentric individualism. There were no doubts
about his loyalty: he was eager, in the disciplined Ignatian
spirit, to do God's will, however it was decided upon by his
superiors. Herein lay their difficulty. The English province of
the Society of Jesus was staffed by intelligent but practical
men, of a higher educational level than the secular Catholic
clergy; many of them were converts from Anglicanism with a
similar background to Hopkins's own. They were working
hard for the sanctification of England in two major areas, both

rapidly expanding: teaching and parish work. Father Hopkins was tried at both, and had no conspicuous success in either. He was at all times treated with great consideration by his superiors, who were kindly if rather unimaginative, but without doubt they found him a difficult case. For his part Hopkins lamented until the end of his life that he was not able to work effectively in the spirit of the Jesuit motto: *ad majoram Dei gloriam* (to the greater glory of God).

Meantime he combined the vocation of the priest with that of the poet. He was never a prolific poet; he wrote in short intense bursts rather than steady composition. And from time to time his old doubts about the reconcilability of poetry with the religious life would recur. In 1881 he expressed these doubts to Richard Watson Dixon, himself a poet and an Anglican clergyman, who returned a blunt and in its way irrefutable response: "Surely one vocation cannot destroy another . . ." (LD 90). But Hopkins had a subtler and more scrupulous mind than Dixon's and he persuasively explained the difficulty. He did, in fact, take the vocation of writing poetry with great seriousness; more seriously, perhaps, than Dixon, who seems not to have thought very deeply about the matter. And for Hopkins fame was a necessary concomitant of being a poet. In an earlier letter to Dixon he had already quoted Milton:

> Fame is the spur that the clear spirit doth raise
> (The last infirmity of noble mind)
> To scorn delights and live laborious days. . . .

Yet though a desirable spur and reward for the poet, fame was a danger for the ordinary Christian, and a positively deadly temptation for the Jesuit. The members of the Society had always been required to avoid any kind of personal fame or distinction, and though many of them, as Dixon pointed out, were men of considerable achievement in art and science, they had always preserved a low profile. Nevertheless, Hopkins did continue as a poet until the end of his life, and extended his creative work into the many remarkable letters of literary criticism and speculation that he wrote to Bridges and Dixon and, after 1883, to Coventry Patmore, these three poets being virtually the only readers of his poetry.

At Mount St. Mary's, Hopkins's first port-of-call after his ordination, he had to cope with a number of odd jobs or what he described to his mother as "a mess of employments," which involved administration, helping the parish priest in the church and acting as a temporary master in the boys' school. In the last capacity Hopkins wrote a farcical prologue to a school production of *Macbeth*, and witnessed the tender affection between two brothers, one acting in a Shrovetide play, one in the audience, which he later commemorated in his poem "Brothers." There, too, he returned to poetry with "The Loss of the *Eurydice*." It was a much more severe and sombre poem than the lyrical sonnets he had written the previous year at St. Beuno's. Although inspired by a shipwreck, it was very different, too, from "The Wreck of the *Deutschland*," even though Hopkins regarded it as a companion piece to the earlier poem. The *Eurydice* was a sailing frigate, returning from a training voyage in fine, clear weather when it was capsized and sunk by a sudden storm in the Channel, on 24th March 1878. Three hundred lives were lost, making this a much greater disaster than the wreck of the *Deutschland*. Among contemporary witnesses of the event was Winston Churchill, then a small child, who remembered seeing the *Eurydice* from the cliffs of the Isle of Wight as it sailed proudly up the Channel, and, after the storm, being shown the floating wreckage and hearing gruesome accounts of drowned seamen. Hopkins's poem is much simpler in fact and appearance than "The Wreck of the *Deutschland*." But it is certainly not a straightforward commemoration of the tragedy; as the poem develops, Hopkins uses the loss of the ship as a figure for the loss of England to the true faith at the Reformation ("with what grace could you, a clergyman of the Church of England, stand godfather to some of the stanzas in that poem," Hopkins asked when Dixon urged him to let it be published in a local newspaper). Formally, too, it is intricate and experimental, if in a less startling way than the earlier poem. Hopkins wrote it at a time when he was still much influenced by the devices of Welsh *cynghanedd*, and this led to some very eccentric rhymes. There is, in fact, an intermittent effect of over-ingenuity and even frigidity, though this is offset by the power and beauty of parts of the poem, such as the lines that haunted Dixon:

> And you were a liar, O blue March day.
> Bright sun lanced fire in the heavenly bay. . . .

Hopkins was not long at Mount St. Mary's. In April 1878, "just when its neighbourhood is gayest and prettiest, as vermilion tiles and orchard blossoms make it," he was called from Derbyshire to the familiar environment of Stonyhurst. There he spent three months coaching students who were working for the External B.A. of London University. Then, in July, he moved to London, to the fashionable Jesuit church of Farm Street, Mayfair. He had been specially asked for by Father Peter Gallway, whom Hopkins had encountered first as a novice-master at Manresa in 1869 and then as Rector of St. Beuno's; Father Gallway was by then Rector of Farm Street, and he continued to regard Hopkins as something of a favourite protégé.

Hopkins thought he was to be stationed permanently at Farm Street, but as he cautiously told Bridges, in a marvellously characteristic phrase, "permanence with us is ginger-bread permanence; cobweb, soapsud, and frost-feather permanence." He was asked to deliver three sermons in August, something of a challenge and an honour, given the nature of the Farm Street congregation, even though at that time of year the smartest of them would have been out of town. In those days preaching was regarded as far more of a formal art—by Catholics as well as Protestants—than it is today, and it was one which Hopkins never properly mastered, though he tried hard enough. He felt that the delivery of the first of his Farm Street sermons was marred by nervousness and flurry, at least at the beginning, though he hoped to do better with the next. Bridges came along to hear his friend preach, but felt obliged to maintain his anti-papist rigour by telling Hopkins afterwards that he had liked neither the music nor the Mass. Hopkins agreed with the first opinion and regretted the second. One account says that Hopkins offended the fashionable congregation by the excessive homeliness of his imagery, when he described the Church as a milch cow wandering through the world, offering grace to humanity from her full udders. The story may be apocryphal, but it does recall Hopkins's perennial difficulty in judging the set of mind of his listeners, whether as a preacher or a lecturer.

Permanence at Farm Street did indeed prove to be "gingerbread permanence." By November he had moved again, this time to become assistant priest at the recently opened parish church of St. Aloysius, Oxford. Hopkins spent a year there, a period when he was over-worked and often in low spirits, though it also coincided with one of his bursts of poetic activity. His return to Oxford would, at best, have required a certain delicate adjustment of his feelings; it was a different world from the one where he had spent four agreeable years as an undergraduate. Physically, the place had changed a good deal in twelve years. There was less of a harmonious contrast between old grey stone buildings and surrounding green meadows, for new suburbs were stretching out around the ancient city. For later generations the rambling Victorian houses of North Oxford—a product of the new dispensation that permitted college fellows to marry and have families—were to acquire a distinct Betjemanesque charm of their own. But for Hopkins they were merely an excrescence. As he wrote in "Duns Scotus's Oxford," one of the poems he composed at this time:

> Thou hast a base and brickish skirt there, sours
> That neighbour-nature thy grey beauty is grounded
> Best in. . . .

Less tangibly, but more importantly, Hopkins was now on the other side of the invisible dividing line that separated "Town" from "Gown," two sides of Oxford that had been frequently at odds ever since the street fights between students and townspeople in the Middle Ages. The church of St. Aloysius was viewed with suspicion by the university authorities as a possible source of subversive Romanist prosletysing among the undergraduates and had been attacked in the press by an ultra-Protestant group. In fact, the parish priest restricted his dealings with the university to pastoral ministrations to the few Catholic undergraduates (a sensitive matter, since from the point of view of the Catholic hierarchy they were not supposed to be there). The main function of the church was simply to provide for the spiritual needs of the Catholics among the townspeople, and Hopkins was kept busy enough. He had to serve the Infirmary, the barracks at Cowley, and to say Mass and preach at the small auxiliary chapel in St. Clement's, on the other side of town, formerly the only Catholic place of worship in Oxford, where Hopkins had attended Mass in his last year as an undergraduate. His work load was made even greater when, shortly before Easter 1879, his superior, Father T. B. Parkinson, broke his collar-bone in a carriage accident, leaving Hopkins to bear single-handed the considerable burden of the Holy Week services. After leaving Oxford he confessed that he did not "quite hit it off with Father Parkinson," a bland, genial priest who had once been an Anglican clergyman and still had something of the air of one; his initials stood for Thomas Brown, but he was known among the Jesuits as Truly Benevolent Parkinson. Nor, indeed, did Hopkins get on particularly well with his congregation, though he tried to. He told Alexander Baillie that he found them "very deserving of affection—though somewhat stiff, stand-off, and depressed" (FL 244). He expressed himself more bluntly to Bridges: "at Oxford every prospect pleases and only man is vile, I mean unsatisfactory to a Catholic missioner" (LB 90). There is a curious and revealing record of Hopkins's time in Oxford in a group photograph of the Oxford Catholic Club taken in front of St. Aloysius's.[1] Father Parkinson sits squarely at his ease in the centre of the picture, surrounded by the young men of the club. Father Hopkins stands on the left of the group, still the short, slight, dapper figure of the undergraduate photographs, but indicating

[1] Reproduced in R. K. R. Thornton, ed., *All My Eyes See: The Visual World of Gerard Manley Hopkins* (Sunderland: 1975), p. 7.

by a certain tenseness in his stance, with his head tilted back at an awkward angle, that he does not feel altogether at ease.

Hopkins's contact with the university world was very limited, but he did see something of friends from his undergraduate days, notably Walter Pater, with whom he exchanged several visits; some months before, Hopkins had been surprised and flattered to hear from Bridges that Pater still remembered and took an interest in him. Unfortunately Hopkins has left no account of what he and Pater talked about on these visits; one would like to know, given Hopkins's possible but uncertain indebtedness to Pater's aesthetic ideas. He also called on T. H. Green, by now Professor of Moral Philosophy. When Green died in 1882 Hopkins expressed the wish that he had seen more of him when he was in Oxford. But the university people he saw most of and in whose company he was happiest were his co-religionists, Francis and Frances de Paravicini. De Paravicini had been a contemporary of Hopkins's at Balliol, and had gone on to become a fellow of the college and lecturer in classics; he was, in fact, one of the first Catholics to become a fellow of an Oxford college, following the relaxation of the religious tests. He and his wife were immensely kind to Hopkins during this period, and he subsequently told de Paravicini: "At Oxford, in my last stay there, I was not happy, but there were many consolations and none pleasanter than what came from you and your house" (FL 62). The de Paravicinis were greatly devoted to Hopkins, and after his death gave a font to St. Aloysius's Church in his memory. By way of diversion Hopkins also found time to attend an illustrated lecture on organ music by the Professor of Music, Sir Gore Ousely, whose name was a great source of amusement to him: "his name in a book of Mallock's would become Sir Bloodclot Reekswell," he told his mother (FL 153).

And despite the pressure of parish duties Hopkins wrote more poems during his months in Oxford than at any time since his outburst of lyrical writing at St. Beuno's two years earlier. I have already referred to one of the best and best-known of these poems, "Duns Scotus's Oxford." Others arose from Hopkins's pastoral duties and showed a concern with

man as well as nature, like "The Bugler's First Communion."
But that nature still touched him deeply we can see in one of
his most poignant lyrics, "Binsey Poplars." He notes its point
of departure in a letter to Dixon, dated 13th March 1879: "I
have been up to Godstow this afternoon. I am sorry to say that
the aspens that lined the river are everyone felled" (LD 26). A
few weeks before Hopkins had read some verses by his father,
lamenting a proposal to fell the trees in Well Walk, Hampstead.

By October Hopkins had moved again. He was told that he
was being transferred to the parish of St. Francis Xavier in
Liverpool, but that he would first have to serve for a time at
Bedford Leigh, near Manchester. Nothing could have been less
like Oxford than this small, gloomy industrial town, but he
conceived an instant affection for the people, and indeed spent
the happiest period of his priesthood there. He told Baillie in
November: "Leigh is a darksome place, with pits and mills
and foundries. Our flock are fervent, I have not seen their
equal" (FL 243). At Leigh he found a rapport with his congregation that had eluded him in the stiffer atmosphere of Oxford.
Lancashire has always been the most intensely Catholic part
of England and there was something in the deep and simple
devotion of the people to which Hopkins instantly warmed.
At Leigh he preached some of his most successful and appreciated sermons, in a direct simple vein. As an example one
can quote from a sermon delivered on 30th November 1879,
on a text from the Epistle to the Romans: "As in the day let
us walk honourably, not in revelry and drunkenness, not in
chambering and wantonness, not in strife and jealousy." Hopkins's words are wonderfully vigorous and lucid, and he clearly
understands the hard, deprived lives of his congregation:

Bad company seem hearty friends, goodnatured companions
and such as a man should have: must not a man have his
friend, his companion, unbend from his work at times, see
company and life? Must he sit mum? must he mope at home?
But, brethren, look at these things nearer. A friend is a
friend, he loves you, he thinks of you and not only of his
own pleasure. A rout of drinking companions do not love

one another, they are selfish, they do not love their own, how can you think they care for strangers? Their own children may be hungry, their mothers or their wives in tears, their homes desolate and they are so good as to spend their time, their money, and their health with you. One of two things: you treat them or they you. If you treat them you like a fool spend your money on the worthless; if they treat you often you are eating their children's bread, you are draining the blood of their little ones. There is no friendship here, no love; there is no love, I say, where nothing comes in but selfishness [SD 41–42].

Bedford Leigh was a short-lived if happy interlude. After spending Christmas at St. Beuno's, where he bathed in the waters of St. Winefred's Well, Hopkins moved on to his "permanent" post at Liverpool; here, indeed, he was to spend over eighteen months, his longest period in any one parish. Liverpool was not very far from Bedford Leigh, and at first Hopkins welcomed what seemed to be the same spirit of Lancastrian Catholic fervour among the people. But before long he came to find Liverpool an oppressively uncongenial environment. He had already experienced the poverty and dirt of an industrial town in Bedford Leigh, but in a city like Liverpool everything was on a larger and grosser scale. Hopkins was, at best, fastidious in his response to his surroundings, and Liverpool came, in a cumulative way, to sicken him. Nor did he find his priestly duties as rewarding as they had been at Bedford Leigh. St. Francis Xavier's was a large, bustling, urban parish, where Hopkins was one of several assistant priests. The church was celebrated for its sermons—regarded as much as performance, even a kind of popular entertainment, as spiritual discourse—and soon after he arrived Hopkins was given the chance to show his quality as a preacher by delivering a series of sermons on Sunday evenings, a time of peak attendance.

He began well enough with a straightforward, moving sermon on the subject "Duty Is Love," very much in the attractively direct vein of the sermons he had preached at Bedford

Leigh. But then he succumbed to a fatal urge to move on to something more elaborate. A similar impulse directed Hopkins's development as a poet, where we see him experimenting, facing and overcoming difficulties, and seldom repeating his effects. But what gave peculiar strength and originality to the poet proved the undoing of the preacher. It is often remarked of Hopkins's poetry that he has two basic manners, which tend in different directions and give a characteristic creative tension to his work: a forceful directness in tone and diction, clashing with a baroque elaboration of form and syntax. The next three sermons Hopkins preached at St. Francis Xavier's were altogether too elaborate, both in idea and in expression. Under the general title of "The Kingdom of God," the trilogy was intended to deal with, successively, God's first kingdom on earth; its glory; and its melancholy fall. It was a subject of great theological subtlety, owing much to Scotus's theory of the Incarnation, which posited that in God's original design Christ would have come to a sinless earth as King and High Priest. In the words of Father Christopher Devlin, editor of Hopkins's sermons: "in this trilogy he embarked with great dialectical detail on a subject which lay near the heart of his poetic philosophy: the lost kingdom of innocence and original justice." Even on the page these sermons demand careful reading, for they have the complex rhetorical and dialectical structure of the great sermons of the seventeenth century, and it is only too easy to believe that the Sunday evening congregation in St. Francis Xavier's, accustomed to direct and sometimes crudely dramatic appeals from the pulpit, could make nothing of such fine speculative exercises. To quote Father Devlin again:

> In a different century or in a different place—say, in a hypothetically Catholic Jacobean Court—one could imagine solemn and sensitive faces, propped on long delicate fingers, watching him with grave intensity. But under the circumstances one can only wonder at the perverse courage which tried to bridge the three-century-widened gap between theology and poetry [SD 6–7].

Even the underlying argument of the sermons was regarded as suspect, or at least susceptible to misunderstanding. Hopkins was not allowed to use his intended title for the last of them, "The Fall of God's First Kingdom," and a blank slip was pasted over it on the printed bills announcing the sermon.

It was several months before Hopkins preached again. He appears to have had useful and well-meant advice from the Rector, Father Clare, about the need to adapt his preaching to the requirements and interests of his listeners. In several later sermons that have been preserved Hopkins reverted to the plain manner that had proved effective at Bedford Leigh. But by a perverse chance some of the best of these were never delivered. And even when he adopted the direct, homely illustrations that he could use so well when he wanted to, Hopkins did not escape censure. On 25th October 1880 he preached a generally admirable sermon on "Divine Providence and the Guardian Angels." He begins by vividly evoking God's intimately loving concern for mankind:

> He takes more interest in a merchant's business than the merchant, in a vessel's steering than the pilot, in a lover's sweetheart than the lover, in a sick man's pain than the sufferer, in our salvation than we ourselves.

One would hardly think that anything here would provoke criticism; nevertheless, Hopkins added a note on the manuscript:

> In consequence of this word *sweetheart* I was in a manner suspended and at all events was forbidden (it was some time after) to preach without having my sermon revised. However when I was going to take the next sermon I had to give after this regulation came into force to Fr. Clare for revision he poohpoohed the matter and would not look at it [SD 89].

Father Clare seems to have been personally well disposed towards Hopkins, but, as Father Devlin suggests, no doubt felt he had to do something about the criticism being directed at this "difficult" assistant, even though he quickly forgot the supposed offence. But one senses an unattractive atmosphere of complaints and petty-mindedness which must have contributed materially to Hopkins's unhappiness. Even the laity did not spare their criticisms. On the manuscript of another sermon he wrote:

> After this sermon one of my penitents told me, with great simplicity, that I was not to be named in the same week with Fr. Clare. "Well," I said "and I will not be named in the same week. But did you hear it all?" He said he did, only that he was sleeping for parts of it [SD 83].

Apart from preaching, Hopkins was involved in the other duties that, then as now, fall to the assistant priest in a large parish: hearing confessions, parish visiting, ministering to the sick. These pastoral duties resulted in one of his greatest poems, dealing with humanity rather than with nature: "Felix Randall," dated April 1880. It seems to have been the only poem that Hopkins wrote in Liverpool: "of all places the most museless" (LD 42). He did, however, write the exquisite "Spring and Fall" at Rose Hill, Lydiate, a few miles outside Liverpool, where he sometimes went to say Mass in the private chapel of the Lightbound family. His always delicate health suffered (many of his disorders would no doubt now be diagnosed as psychosomatic in origin), and in September 1880 he complained to Bridges of suffering from diarrhoea and vomiting brought on by a combination of heat and long hours spent in the confessional. The following month fatigue and discouragement led to an outburst of extreme bitterness:

> I daresay you have long expected as you have long deserved an answer to your last kind and cheering—let us say, number or issue. But I could never write; time and spirits were wanting; one is so fagged, so harried and gallied up and down. And the drunkards go on drinking, the filthy, as the scripture says, are filthy still: human nature is so inveterate. Would that I had seen the last of it [LB 110].

It was only after he had left Liverpool that Hopkins was able to transcend his revulsion and give a more measured account of his experiences. He wrote to Dixon in December 1881:

> My Liverpool and Glasgow experience laid upon my mind a conviction, a truly crushing conviction, of the misery of town life to the poor and more than to the poor, of the misery of the poor in general, of the degradation even of our race, of the hollowness of this century's civilization: it made even life a burden to me to have daily thrust upon me the things I saw [LD 97].

Here Hopkins is writing in the tradition of earlier Victorian critics of industrial civilization—Ruskin and Carlyle, Dickens and Mrs. Gaskell—and recalling the radical sentiments of his "red letter" to Bridges in 1871. But his political attitudes were becoming steadily more Conservative. In April 1880 he described himself as gloomy about the recent elections, when Gladstone and the Liberal Party had unexpectedly returned to office (FL 157). The following year he was scandalized by the battle of Majuba in South Africa, when British troops were soundly beaten by the Boers, and reflected: "Would that we had some great statesman, a patriot and not a truckler to Russia or the Freemasons" (FL 158). During the rest of Hopkins's life a rather strident imperialism and an obsessive abuse of Gladstone recur in his letters. He was encouraged by the fact that of his regular correspondents, Bridges and Dixon were staunch Tories, while Patmore was more extreme, a reactionary of a quite bizarre kind. Hopkins's concern for the miseries of the poor was genuine enough, but his solution was not socialism but an idealistic Tory radicalism.

Eventually his long, weary period at Liverpool came to an end. Not long before he left he remarked with feeling to Bridges: "You give me a long jobation about eccentricities. Alas, I have heard so much about and suffered so much for and in fact been completely ruined for life by my alleged singularities that they are a sore subject" (LB 126). It was a burden Hopkins was to bear until the end of his life. In August

1881 he was sent on supply to a parish in Glasgow; expecting to stay only a fortnight, he was there for two months. Glasgow was another grim city, but he preferred it to Liverpool. He seems to have had some leisure there, for he wrote several long letters to Dixon; a trip to the Highlands in September produced "Inversnaid," and on Loch Lomond he "jotted down" a musical setting of one of Dixon's poems. Then, in October, he travelled south, back to Manresa House where he had begun his life as a Jesuit, thirteen years before. He was in every sense returning to his origins, since he was embarking on the "tertianship" or "second novitiate," a ten-month period of prayer, study, contemplation and manual work, indoors and outdoors, which the Jesuit had to complete before he could take his final vows in the order. The tertian had in fact to live in the same simple, circumscribed way as the novices, whatever his previous status and activities in the order. On 16th September Hopkins wrote to Bridges from Glasgow:

> Things are pleasanter here than at Liverpool. Wretched place too Glasgow is, like all our great towns; still I get on better here, though bad is the best of my getting on. But now I feel that I need the noviceship very much and shall be every way better off when I have been made more spiritual minded [LB 135].

At Roehampton Hopkins found both peace of spirit and, after two years in industrial towns, relief for the senses in the rural surroundings: "This spot, though it has suffered much from decay of nature and more from the hand of man, is still beautiful. It is besides a great rest to be here and I am in a very contented frame of mind" [LB 138].

That autumn Hopkins made, once more, the thirty-day Long Retreat based on St. Ignatius's Spiritual Exercises. His extensive retreat notes are reproduced in the *Sermons and Devotional Writings* with Father Devlin's helpful comments. In them we see Hopkins elaborating on St. Ignatius's bluntly practical directives with his own refinements of Scotist subtlety. During the tertianship secular reading and writing were restricted;

Hopkins wrote no poetry but kept up his correspondence with Bridges and Dixon on his periodical free days. In January he had a momentary scare that he would have to return to Liverpool; one of the assistant priests at St. Francis Xavier's had died suddenly and Hopkins was certain he would be sent for to take his place. But this did not come about. On 1st February 1882 he wrote to Bridges: "I find the life trying—weakening, I mean. But the calm of mind is delightful: I am afraid I shall leave it behind" (LB 141). A few weeks later he did move north again for a while. The rules of the tertianship required the priest undergoing it to take part in a special parish mission. On 3rd April Hopkins wrote again to Bridges, who was recovering from a long and dangerous illness; he was then at St. Wilfrid's Church, Preston, Lancashire:

> At the beginning of Lent I came from Roehampton here to stop a gap and do some parish work; I then went to Maryport on the coast of Cumberland to take part in a Mission, which is something like a Revival without the hysteria and the heresy, and it had the effect of bringing me out and making me speak very plainly and strongly (I enjoyed that, for I dearly like calling a spade a spade): it was the first thing of the sort I had been employed in; but no more of this now [LB 143].

Hopkins may have learnt from his painful experiences in Liverpool how to "speak very plainly and strongly." He returned to Roehampton, and in May was visited by Bridges, now fully recovered, accompanied by a small nephew. On this visit some small awkwardness arose, seemingly prompted by Hopkins's inveterate scrupulosity. Bridges had wanted to buy some peaches and the gardener had been very willing to sell them. But for some reason Hopkins dissuaded his friend from the purchase. It was a small incident but it stuck in Bridges's mind, and nearly fifty years later he recalled it in *The Testament of Beauty*. He had offered a peach to Hopkins, who did not want to accept:

> And so
> When the young poet my companion in study
> and friend of my heart refused a peach at my hands,
> he being then a housecarl in Loyola's menie,
> 'twas that he fear'd the savour of it, and when he waived
> his scruple to my banter, 'twas to avoid offence.
>
> [III, 433–38]

Following a further retreat of seven days, Hopkins took his final vows in the Society of Jesus, at a ceremony during the nine o'clock Mass on 15th August, the feast of the Assumption. Right up to the end of his time at Manresa he actively engaged in spiritual writing. As he told Bridges:

> I did in my last week at Roehampton write 16 pages of a rough draft of a commentary on St. Ignatius's Spiritual Exercises. This work would interest none but a Jesuit, but to me it is interesting enough and, as you see, it is very professional [LB 150].

Hopkins never returned to parish work, apart from occasional short periods on supply or to help out at busy times of the year. It was decided he would be better employed in teaching, and with this in view he returned to Stonyhurst in September 1882 to take up the kind of work he had briefly engaged in during the spring of 1878: teaching Latin and Greek to candidates for the London External B.A. The Jesuit Provincial was sympathetic to Hopkins's plans for literary and scholarly works, and wanted him to devote his spare time to them. He was not short of projects: there was a "great ode" on the Elizabethan Jesuit martyr, Edmund Campion, and a verse drama about St. Winefred, which he had started in 1879. And he was newly fired with the idea of writing a book on Greek lyric poetry. But these schemes came to nothing, or at best remained in fragments. In January 1883 Hopkins wrote to Baillie in a kind of spirited gloom:

> I like my pupils and do not wholly dislike the work, but I fall into or continue in a heavy weary state of body and mind in which my go is gone (the elegance of that phrase!

as Thackeray says, it makes one think what vast sums must have been spent on my education!) I make no way with what I read, and seem but half a man. It is a sad thing to say. I try, and am even meant to try, in my spare time (and if I were fresher or if it were anyone but myself there would be a good deal of spare time taking short and long together) to write some books; but I find myself so tired or so harassed I fear they will be never written [FL 251–52].

Hopkins wrote only few poems during this time at Stony-hurst, but they are among his most original works, particularly "The Leaden Echo and the Golden Echo." The manuscript is dated 13th October 1882, though it may have been written earlier. This poem is the most impressive surviving portion of the abandoned tragedy "St. Winefred's Well," where it was to have been a "maidens' song." Hopkins later told Dixon: "I never did anything more musical," and the poem is indeed a remarkable instance of poetry verging on music whilst remaining charged with meaning. The other fragments that remain of "St. Winefred's Well" contain powerful lines, but suggest that the whole work, if ever finished, was not likely to have been any more of a theatrical success than the many other verse dramas produced by Victorian poets. Hopkins acknowledged that he lacked Shakespeare's practical experience of the theatre, though he insisted that "St. Winefred's Well" was to be a play and not a dramatic poem. In May 1883, as part of the Stonyhurst custom of honouring Mary in the month of May, Hopkins wrote "The Blessed Virgin compared to the Air we Breathe," an idiosyncratic and baroque treatment of a conventional topic. Five years before, on the same occasion, he had written "The May Magnificat." He also wrote a sonnet, "Ribblesdale," whose genesis may lie in a description of the surrounding country that he made soon after his arrival. Giving an account of the new college building, he added: "There are acres of flat roof which, when the air is not thick, as unhappily it mostly is, commands a noble view of this Lancashire landscape, Pendle Hill, Ribblesdale, the fells, and all round, bleakish but solemn and beautiful" (LB 151). "Ribblesdale" catches this sense of a severe, bleak beauty. One should also mention Hopkins's venture into light verse with a set of three comic triolets published in *The Stonyhurst Magazine* in March 1883. Hopkins deprecatingly told Bridges: "they have the taint of jest and dare not meet your eye" (LB 178), though he did after all send them. Hopkins is no doubt satirising the contemporary cult of the triolet and similar old French verse forms associated with Austin Dobson and other minor poets. In the most accomplished of the three, "The Child is Father to the Man," Hopkins recoils in sardonic amazement from the often-quoted Wordsworthian sentiment.

Although Hopkins wrote little poetry at Stonyhurst, and soon complained of being unable to make much progress with his book on the Greek lyric, he still directed his flagging energies into new channels. It is a feature of Hopkins's later years that whilst always lamenting his fatigue and inability to cope with his proper work, he constantly distracted himself with new proposals and interests. Thus, at Stonyhurst he tried to "get in a bit of strumming" on the piano every day. He was tackling Bach's fugues and begged Bridges to send him some Purcell. Ever since his time at Liverpool Hopkins had struggled in an uncertain, self-taught way to compose music. A friend of Bridges's offered expert criticism of one of his compositions, upon which Hopkins, characteristically, argued back. He also started to learn Anglo-Saxon and found it "a vastly superior thing to what we have now." Another new interest, or perhaps a development of an old one, is apparent in several letters that Hopkins contributed to the scientific weekly, *Nature*. In November 1882 and again in November 1883 he sent letters describing curious phenomena caused by cloud-shadows in the eastern sky at sunset. Here Hopkins reverts to the Ruskinian interest in the scientific-cum-aesthetic aspects of visual perception that had informed so many of his journal entries. Then, on 3rd January 1884, he contributed a long and detailed letter describing the remarkable sunsets that had been recently visible, the result of the world-wide distribution of dust in the upper atmosphere following the explosion of the volcanic island of Krakatoa in the East Indies. Even in such a severely scientific context Hopkins's descriptive manner is unmistakable.

> The glow is intense, this is what strikes everyone; it has prolonged the daylight, and optically changed the season; it bathes the whole sky, it is mistaken for the reflection of a great fire; at the sundown itself and southwards from that on December 4th, I took a note of it as more like inflamed flesh than the lucid reds of ordinary sunsets. On the same evening the fields facing west glowed as if overlaid with yellow wax [LD 163].

About this time Hopkins evolved another project, to write a commentary on Newman's philosophical treatise, *A Grammar of Assent*, though he had been quite critical when he first read it in 1873. He put the idea to Newman in a letter of February 1883, as part of his annual birthday greeting to the Cardinal. He shortly received a reply, which though written with all the exquisite tact and courtesy of which Newman was capable, was a firm rejection of the proposal. No more was heard of it.

Later that year Hopkins made a new friend. The end of the scholastic year at Stonyhurst was marked by a "Great Academy," or speech-day, to which distinguished guests were invited. Among them, that year, was Coventry Patmore, at that time a middle-aged Catholic poet of considerable reputation as the author, many years before, of *The Angel in the House*. Hopkins had known and admired Patmore's poetry ever since he was an undergraduate, and must have been delighted when the Rector of Stonyhurst asked him to look after the visitor during his three days at the college. "I saw a good deal of him and had a good deal of talk," he wrote (LD 111). Patmore did not then know that Hopkins was himself a poet, but he must have been impressed with his companion's manifest intelligence and literary knowledge and sensibility. Patmore knew and liked what he had seen of Bridges's poetry, but had never encountered Canon Dixon's; he responded with great enthusiasm when Hopkins showed him copies of Dixon's poems. During their days together Hopkins offered—in what way, or under what prompting is not clear—to help Patmore revise his poems for a new collected edition. Patmore welcomed the offer. Hopkins then left Stonyhurst for the summer vacation. After a brief visit to Holland with his parents—his first trip abroad since his Alpine tour in 1868—he embarked on a copious correspondence with Patmore: detailed, painstaking, enthusiastic on his part, stiff and laconic, though appreciative, on Patmore's.

Hopkins, it is often justly remarked, was a great letter-writer; or, more exactly, a great literary letter-writer. He belongs to that small company of writers whose letters offer both a vivid revelation of a unique personality and valuable literary criticism, the two elements inseparably bound together. One thinks of Keats, of Henry James, of D. H. Lawrence. His correspondence with Bridges and Dixon, and then with Patmore, shows that though Hopkins was only intermittently a poet from 1875 to the end of his life, he was consistently a literary critic. Hopkins's abilities as a critic were, indeed, an aspect of his genius as a poet. To succeed as a poet one needs not only creativity, inspiration, or whatever one calls it, but also the capacity to weigh words, to choose, to revise or reject. Hopkins had this capacity to a fine degree, as the drafts of his poems show, and it was this that made him so sensitive a reader of his friends' poetry. There are few parallels in the history of literature; the closest is, perhaps, Ezra Pound's creative revision of the drafts of *The Waste Land*. The three poets to whose work Hopkins devoted so much critical care and love are now little read, so his comments on them are not consistently interesting. Hopkins today is most rewarding as a critic in his casual but searching judgments on his contemporaries, his reassessments of major works of the past and his speculations on the theory of literature.

His correspondence with Bridges and Dixon was far more than a detached exercise in literary criticism. His letters to these two men (his friendship with Bridges had to be largely epistolary in later years, and that with Dixon almost entirely so) represented the maintenance of friendships that he found immensely sustaining in the midst of the difficulties and discouragements of his priestly life. He had the satisfaction of putting Bridges and Dixon in touch with each other and a firm friendship developed between them. Early in this century Dixon was the first of the three dead friends whose poetry appeared in collections that Bridges edited; the second was Digby Mackworth Dolben and the third was Hopkins himself.

These friendships perhaps deserve a slightly fuller account than I have so far given. At Oxford Hopkins and Bridges had been good friends, though perhaps no better than Hopkins and several other of his contemporaries. Yet their friendship endured remarkably. After a long break following Hopkins's "red letter" in 1871, they resumed correspondence, particularly after Hopkins realised that his friend was now a published poet. Thereafter Hopkins subjected Bridges's poems, published or unpublished, to close criticism. There was a good deal of argument between them, though it is inevitably one-sided in survival since Bridges's letters unfortunately have been lost. Generally Bridges seems to have welcomed Hopkins's criticisms, many of which were very constructive, though sometimes he seemed disconcerted by them. In October 1879 Hopkins was distressed when Bridges asked him whether he really thought there was any good in his going on writing poetry. Hopkins assured his friend of his admiration for his work, and indicated something of his critical method: "It is just as if I had written it myself and were dissatisfied, as you know that in the process of composition one almost always is, before things reach their final form" (LB 94). Hopkins rarely qualified or muffled his judgments, particularly when writing to so old a friend as Bridges, and it is this directness of utterance that gives his correspondence its flavour, however chilling it must sometimes have been for the recipient. One may quote his judgment on one of Bridges's best-known poems, a shrewd and exuberant piece of criticism:

> The Dead Child is a fine poem, I am aware, but I am not bound to like it best; I do not in fact like it best nor think it the best you have written, as you say it is. I do not think either the rhythm or the thought flowing enough. The diction

is not exquisite, as yours can be when you are at ease. No, but you say it is severe: perhaps it is bald. But indeed "wise, sad head" and "firm, pale hands" do not strike me as severe at all, nor yet exquisite. Rather they belong to a familiar commonplace about "Reader, have you never hung over the pillow of . . . pallid cheek, clammy brow . . . long, long night-watches . . . surely, Sir Josiah Bickerstaff, there is *some* hope! O say not all is over. It cannot be"—You know [LB 122].

It appears that Bridges was no less forthright. One of the most valuable aspects of the correspondence is the way in which Hopkins, retorting to Bridges's criticisms, was provoked into providing extended explanations of what he was trying to do, particularly with his first experiments, like "The Wreck of the *Deutschland*" and "The Loss of the *Eurydice*." Without succumbing to the intentional fallacy, we can be grateful for these detailed accounts of Hopkins's poetic aims. One of Hopkins's most interesting letters, and of a less narrowly technical kind than many, was sent to Bridges from Stonyhurst on 18th October 1882. Bridges had suggested that Hopkins might have been influenced by Whitman in "The Leaden Echo and the Golden Echo." In his reply Hopkins proceeds logically by first saying how little of Whitman he has read, next acknowledging that even a small amount of such original poetry as Whitman's might well be influential, and then finally showing at length just how unlike Whitman's prosody is his own. But the most interesting aspect of the letter is a casual paragraph near the beginning:

But first I may as well say what I should not otherwise have said, that I always knew in my heart Walt Whitman's mind to be more like my own than any other man's living. As he is a very great scoundrel this is not a pleasant confession. And this also makes me the more desirous to read him and the more determined that I will not [LB 155].

This confession is intriguing but puzzling. It may be that Hopkins responded warmly to Whitman's generosity of spirit and rhapsodic largeness; perhaps, too, it has been suggested, he felt a covert sympathy with Whitman's homosexual inclinations, though how far these were recognised as such at the time is questionable. But one can quote Hopkins's later remark to Bridges, when he sent him the manuscript of "Harry Ploughman": "when you read it let me know if there is anything like it in Walt Whitman, as perhaps there may be, and I should be sorry for that" (LB 262). Some such perturbation may have led Hopkins to describe Whitman so confidently as a "very great scoundrel"; but he may also have been politically scandalized by Whitman's republicanism and egalitarianism.

Such moments of self-revelation are uncommon in the correspondence. For the most part Hopkins stays close to the technical, rhetorical or prosodic elements of literary discussion, and avoids those larger areas where discussion of "literature" is hardly to be distinguished from discussion of "life." For all their mutual affection Bridges and Hopkins were at odds on fundamental questions, above all on religion. Bridges's attitude to Catholicism seems to have been at best uncomprehending, at worst hostile; this much is apparent in his notes to Hopkins's *Poems*. And he seems to have had a somewhat insensitive way of needling Hopkins on religious questions. Hopkins for his part occasionally upbraided Bridges for his apparent lack of proper religious convictions; as far as Hopkins was concerned, religion was, in the end, far more important than literature. In 1879 he wrote: "When we met in London we never but once, and then only for a few minutes before parting, spoke on any important subject, but always on literature. This I regret very much" (LB 60). He then accuses Bridges of making insufficient effort in pursuing spiritual truth, and tells him that he will be helped by a certain amount of self-denial, particularly in alms-giving, which benefits both the giver and the recipient: "I am now talking pure Christianity, as you may remember, but also I am talking pure sense as you must see." He concludes with the half-apologetic reflection: "I feel it is very bold, as it is uncalled for, of me to have written the above. Still, if we care for fine verses how much more for a noble life!" Bridges seems to have taken this advice very badly and to have deliberately or carelessly misunderstood what Hopkins was trying to tell him. In his reply he alleged that Hopkins was urging him to excesses of self-mortifying asceticism, which was certainly not the case, as Hopkins had to explain in a further letter.

Three years later Hopkins writes in some exasperation, apropos of a Corpus Christi procession that Bridges had watched at Roehampton:

> It is long since such things had any significance for you. But what is strange and unpleasant is that you sometimes speak as if they had in reality none for me and you were waiting with a certain disgust till I too should be disgusted with myself enough to throw off the mask. . . . Yet I can hardly think you do not think I am not in earnest. And let me say, to take no higher ground, that without earnestness there is nothing sound or beautiful in character and that a cynical vein much indulged in coarsens everything in us. Not that you do overindulge this vein in other matters: why then does it bulk out in that diseased and varicose way in this? [LB 148].

Other readers since Bridges have had difficulty in understanding how, given Hopkins's breadth of interests and intellectual independence, and his quick, probing critical spirit, he could really have believed what he did. But as his co-religionist, Coventry Patmore, also an independent-minded man in his own way, wrote after Hopkins's death: "Gerard Hopkins was the only orthodox, and as far as I could see, saintly man in whom religion had absolutely no narrowing effect upon his general opinions and sympathies" (FL xxxvi). With so many possibilities of disagreement and misunderstanding, it is not surprising that Hopkins and Bridges generally restricted their correspondence to precisely literary questions where argument, however spirited at times, could be contained and limited. Even here, Hopkins could be put out by Bridges's way of doing things. Thus, when Bridges's poem, *Prometheus the Firegiver*, came out in what was for those days a rather costly limited edition, Hopkins complained to Dixon:

This private printing of *Prometheus* may turn out un-
fortunate. I have myself no taste for what is called dainty in
the get up of books and am altogether wanting in the spirit
of a bookhunter. 10s seems like what is called a prohibitive
price. I could not recommend our library to get such a book
and till the second edition I shall not see the poem in print
[LD 107].

Again, when in 1882 Bridges gave up medicine and retired to
a country house at Yattenden in Berkshire to devote himself to
writing, Hopkins expressed what would nowadays be called
social concern: "I should be sorry to think you did nothing
down there but literary work: could you not be a magistrate?
This would be honourable and valuable public duty. Consider
it" (LB 152). But the friendship continued unaffected until the
end; indeed, the one surviving letter from Bridges was written
during Hopkins's final illness in May 1889. And as I have
already remarked, Hopkins's survival as a poet is because of
Bridges's careful custodianship of his manuscripts.

There were no contentious subjects or even much clash of
opinion in Hopkins's correspondence with Canon Dixon, though
it contains some of his most important literary criticism.
Richard Watson Dixon was eleven years older than Hopkins,
and as a young man had played some part in the Pre-Raphaelite
movement. He had been at school with the painter Edward
Burne-Jones, and they went on to be undergraduates at Oxford
together. There they met the young William Morris, and the
three formed a group of keen medievalists known as "The
Brotherhood," not to be confused with the original Pre-
Raphaelite Brotherhood of 1848. They produced *The Oxford
and Cambridge* magazine, and later on Burne-Jones and Morris
introduced themselves to Rossetti and were caught up in the
Pre-Raphaelite mainstream. They took part in the celebrated
adventure, instigated by Rossetti, of painting murals in the
Oxford Union building in 1857. The young artists had more
enthusiasm than experience, and, being totally ignorant of
fresco technique, neglected to prepare the walls first; as a

result the murals started to fade almost as soon as they were finished. It was, though, a significant moment in the development of Pre-Raphaelitism. Dixon was a poet rather than a painter but he is said to have wielded a paintbrush in the Union along with the rest of them. Then, in 1858, he was ordained in the Church of England. He became a curate at a parish in Lambeth, South London, but travelled to Oxford the following year in order to officiate at the marriage of William Morris and the legendarily beautiful Jane Burden. In 1861 Dixon published a collection of poems, *Christ's Company*, and it was in this year that Hopkins first met him, when Dixon was acting for a few months as a master at Highgate School. Hopkins heard something about *Christ's Company* from another master and when he was at Oxford he read the book, though he left no account of his reaction to it. He did, however, jot down Dixon's name on three occasions in his undergraduate notebooks; once in a list of Pre-Raphaelites and once in a list of "Oxford poets." In the last entry, in 1866, Hopkins wrote down Dixon's address as well, as if he might want to write to him. But the intention, if entertained, was not acted on for many years. To say that Dixon's later career was uneventful is almost an understatement. He moved to Cumberland in the far north of England and became a schoolmaster, then a minor canon and honorary librarian of Carlisle Cathedral and eventually vicar of the village of Hayton. He continued to be a fairly prolific if neglected poet, and in 1864 published a second volume, *Historical Odes*. By temperament a scholar as well as a poet, he embarked at Hayton on a long work of ecclesiastical history, a study in several volumes of the development of the Church of England in the middle years of the sixteenth century following the Reformation. It was this work that eventually gained for Dixon such academic recognition as he attained during his lifetime—a doctorate of divinity at Oxford and a fellowship of his old college—though not until just before his death in 1900. His scholarship received no encouragement in his lifetime from his ecclesiastical superiors; being only an honorary canon, he had to devote most of his time to parish work instead of benefiting from the greater leisure that might have come from a cathedral appointment. As the writer of the entry in the *Dictionary of National Biography* puts it: "His friends would have greatly valued for him the increase of leisure and opportunities for study which a cathedral stall would have offered, but it was not to be." In the circumstances Dixon's achievement in historical scholarship was remarkable.

As a man Dixon appears as an attractive but dim figure. There was a gentle, loveable quality about him that inspired great devotion in his few friends, particularly Bridges in later years. It has been his misfortune to be remembered not so much for his own sake as for his accounts of other and larger figures in whose lives he played some part, like Morris, Rossetti, Burne-Jones (who remained a life-long friend) and Hopkins. If few people read Dixon's poetry in his lifetime, one can safely say that even fewer do so today, for none of it has been reprinted since Bridges's selection came out in 1909. There is, however, a representative selection in the *Oxford Book of Nineteenth Century Verse*, and in 1962 James Sambrook published a sympathetic and informative life of Dixon, *A Poet Hidden*. The writer of the *D.N.B.* entry on Dixon noted: "The poems of the first volume, though largely upon religious subjects, are not strictly religious poetry: they are works of picturesque imagination rather than of devotional feeling." The "picturesque imagination" is heavily Pre-Raphaelite, as we see in such lines as these from "St. Mary Magadalen," which have the flat, decorative quality both of Rossetti's early paintings and much of Morris's poetry:

> Kneeling before the altar step
>   Her white face stretched above her hands;
> In one great line her body thin
> Rose robed right upwards to her chin;
> Her hair rebelled in golden bands,
>   And filled her hands.

Dixon is perhaps at his best in the beautiful lyric, "The Feathers of the Willow," which is individual and memorable:

The feathers of the willow
Are half of them grown yellow
　　Above the swelling stream;
And ragged are the bushes,
And rusty now the rushes,
　　And wild the clouded gleam.

The thistle now is older,
His stalk begins to moulder,
　　His head is white as snow;
The branches all are barer,
The linnet's song is rarer,
　　The robin pipeth now.

This was one of the poems that Hopkins singled out for praise when, quite unexpectedly, he wrote to Dixon in June 1878, during his brief period at Stonyhurst between Mount St. Mary's and Farm Street. He reminded Dixon of their former acquaintance at Highgate, though he doubted if Dixon would remember him, and went on to say how much Dixon's poetry meant to him at Oxford and subsequently: "I introduced your poems to my friends and, if they did not share my own enthusiasm, made them at all events admire." It was evidently this enthusiasm that prompted the laconic entries in Hopkins's Oxford notebooks. There are no references to Dixon in Hopkins's subsequent journals or correspondence, and his letter to Dixon in 1878 was on a sudden impulse, after he read a review of the first volume of Dixon's *History of the Church of England*. Seeing this evidence of Dixon's continuing activity, he finally wrote to him, something he might have done at any time in the intervening years, as he tells the older man. He tells Dixon how he copied out some of his favourite poems when he entered the Society of Jesus and could take no books of his own, says something about his continuing admiration and regrets that the poems are not better known. This letter not only gratified Dixon, it amazed and even stunned him; he was at first unable to reply, so various were the emotions that it provoked. Having resigned himself to general neglect as a poet, he now received unexpected assurance that someone had long admired his work and could write about it with warm if discriminating praise. In his reply Dixon said how deeply moved he had been by Hopkins's letter, and added that he thought he could remember him at Highgate School: "At least I remember a pale young boy, very light and active, with a very meditative & intellectual face, whose name, if I am not vastly mistaken, was yours" (LD 4).

Thenceforth a regular and sometimes copious correspondence ensued between the two men. In his next letter Hopkins recommended Bridges's poems to Dixon and engaged in some energetic reflections about the nature of poetic fame, boldly asserting an idea that dominated his understanding of both poetry and religion: "The only just judge, the only just literary critic, is Christ, who prizes, is proud of, and admires, more than any man, more than the receiver himself can, the gifts of his own making" (LD 8). In his reply Dixon said of this sentence: "I have drawn deep consolation from that: it came upon me with the force of a revelation" (LD 10). Dixon was to acknowledge himself similarly impressed with observations by Hopkins throughout the correspondence; there was no doubt in his mind that his onetime pupil had a subtler and more powerful intellect. He also acknowledged that Hopkins's commitment to the religious life was of a more conscious and intense kind than his own; hence the discussion between them, to which I have already referred, about the reconcilability of the vocations of priest and poet. The question of poetic fame was at the heart of Hopkins's difficulty; he saw it as desirable for the poet and undesirable for the priest, or at least for the Jesuit, hence his reluctance to attempt publication following his two rebuffs from *The Month*. On this point Dixon pressed him quite hard. He discovered in time that Hopkins was a poet and asked to see some of his manuscript poems. His response was warmly enthusiastic rather than carefully critical, and it is doubtful if he really made much of "The Wreck of the *Deutschland*." Then, in December 1879, he wrote to Hopkins asking if he might send "The Loss of the *Eurydice*" to one of the newspapers in Carlisle, together with a few words of introduction. Hopkins found many reasons for being appalled at the idea and he forbade Dixon to do any such thing, however grateful he was for Dixon's "warmhearted but much mistaken kindness." In 1881 Dixon tried again. He had been approached by Hall Caine, a friend and later biographer of Rossetti, to ask if he might reprint two of Dixon's sonnets in a large anthology of sonnets he was compiling; Caine also asked if Dixon knew of any good unpublished sonnets that might go into the collection. Dixon had told Caine about Hopkins, indeed shown him two of his sonnets, and he urged Hopkins to submit something. This time Hopkins overcame his repugnance towards the idea of publication and sent Caine three sonnets. But he was not particularly surprised, nor disappointed, when Hall Caine rejected the sonnets (one of them was "Andromeda," the others are not identified) with the explanation that the purpose of his anthology was "to demonstrate the impossibility of improving upon the acknowledged structure whether as to rhyme-scheme or measure." Bridges, who had also been approached, was indignant at this rejection and refused to allow any of his own sonnets to appear in the collection, despite Hopkins's protests.

The correspondence of Hopkins and Dixon is almost entirely literary, without the hint and occasional obtrusion of more personal pressures and interests that gives a certain sharpness to the letters between Hopkins and Bridges. Writing to his new correspondent, Hopkins explains such things as his interest in Milton's prosody and what he understands by "sprung rhythm." He reads Dixon's unpublished poems with the same close critical attention he gave to Bridges's. Hopkins is in time a little more reserved, less openly enthusiastic about Dixon's poetry than he had been in his first letter, though he still gives praise wherever he feels it is due. It may be that when he wrote to Dixon in 1878 he was expressing what he had felt as a very young man rather than stating his more mature feelings. Nevertheless, Dixon remained generally grateful for Hopkins's care and suggestions, even if they sometimes struck him as over-subtle. He might well have thought so about the analysis of his narrative poem, "Love's Casuistry," which Hopkins sees as ending up like a chess-problem and illustrates with a quasi-algebraic diagram (LD 79), curiously anticipating the kind of thing one finds today in structuralist analyses.

More rewarding are the general literary discussions between the two poets, where Dixon makes his own quite valuable contributions. The correspondence is particularly interesting as an illustration of the shift of literary taste away from the Victorian giants that began about 1880. Neither of them has much time for Browning, for instance; he provoked one of Hopkins's most spirited critical fancies:

> Now he has got a great deal of what came in with Kingsley and the Broad Church school, a way of talking (and making his people talk) with the air and spirit of a man bouncing up from the table with his mouth full of bread and cheese and saying that he meant to stand no blasted nonsense [LD 74].

This, of course, is very far from being the whole truth about Browning; but it does define an aspect of Browning, one which readers were beginning to tire of at that time. If anything Dixon tends to be more severe in his rejections than Hopkins. Despite his early admiration for Tennyson, Dixon sees little to admire in the later work and concludes: "Tennyson is a great outsider" (LD 19). Hopkins cannot go so far: "I feel what you mean, though it grieves me to hear him deprecated, as of late has often been done. Come what may he will be one of our greatest poets" (LD 24). Even so, Hopkins totally rejects such an immensely popular work as the *Idylls of the King:* "He shd. have called them *Charades from the Middle Ages* (dedicated by permission to H.R.H. etc)" (LD 24). Again, Dixon is very hostile to Carlyle: "He was the greatest imposter, I think, that ever figured in literature: so great that it required his own hand to expose him" (LD 60). Hopkins can only agree up to a point: "I always thought him morally an imposter, worst of all imposters a false prophet. And his style has imposture or pretence in it. But I find it difficult to think there is imposture in his genius itself" (LD 75).

Inevitably Hopkins and Dixon wanted to meet, but this proved extraordinarily difficult to arrange. Bridges, whom Hopkins had put into touch with Dixon, travelled to Hayton to visit him in 1880, and has left a pleasant account of his first impression of the Canon on the station as "a tallish, elderly figure, its litheness lost in a slight scholarly stoop . . . wearing unimpeachable black cloth negligently, and a low-crowned clerical hat banded with twisted silk" (LD xiii). But Hopkins did not have the same freedom to travel. He had hoped to visit Hayton on his journey south from Glasgow in the autumn of 1881, but it could not, in the end, be arranged, much to the regret of both of them. Finally, though, they contrived a brief meeting. In March 1882 Hopkins completed his period as a missioner at Maryport, Cumberland, and had to return to Preston via Carlisle. He had about three and a half hours to wait between trains, and there, on 27th March, Hopkins and Dixon met for the first time since the days at Highgate School over twenty years before. They had lunch together and visited Carlisle Cathedral. Dixon at once recognised "the pale young boy, very light and active" in the Jesuit priest, but it was a rather constrained occasion. Dixon was, as he later freely acknowledged, shy, and there was not time for the shyness to wear off. Writing to Bridges, Hopkins gave a detached account of the meeting:

> Partly through this sightseeing and more through shyness on his part (not on mine) we did not get much intimate or even interesting talk. I was amused when his hat twice blew off in English Street to watch his behaviour. I wish I could have been with him longer [LB 144].

There were no further opportunities to deepen their personal intimacy, for as far as is known, Hopkins and Dixon never met again. But their correspondence continued as warmly as ever. It was a true friendship, even if circumstances restricted it to letters.

In the summer of 1883 Hopkins had been back at Stonyhurst for a year. Although, given his anxieties and nervous disorders, it would be an exaggeration to say that he was happy there, he was at least in comfortable and familiar surroundings, with some agreeable and cultivated colleagues among the other priests of the community. And, as he admitted, his work was not really heavy. However, he had no reason to believe that he would be kept there much longer: as always he had to contend with "ginger-bread permanence; cobweb, soapsud, and frost-feather permanence." In July he wrote to Bridges, perhaps alluding to some famous lines from *The Duchess of Malfi* ("We are merely the stars' tennis-balls, struck and bandied Which way please them"): "I have long been Fortune's football and am blowing up the bladder of resolution big and buxom for another kick of her foot. I shall be sorry to leave Stonyhurst; but go or stay there is no likelihood of my ever doing anything to last" (LB 183). It seemed that the kick was to be averted, for Hopkins shortly heard that his appointment had been renewed for a further year. But a few months later it was, after all, delivered, and all the more vehemently for the brief reprieve.

5

The Dublin Years

IN FEBRUARY 1884 Hopkins moved from Stonyhurst to Dublin.
He now had a new and resounding title: Fellow of the
Royal University of Ireland and Professor of Greek at University College, Dublin. It seemed as if the Society of Jesus
had at last found an honourable and appropriate position for
the brilliant but "difficult" Father Hopkins. He recognised the
honour but, from the beginning, had misgivings. In his annual
birthday letter to Newman he wrote:

> I am writing from where I never thought to be, in a Univer-
> sity for Catholic Ireland begun under your leadership, which
> has since those days indeed long and unhappily languished,
> but for which we now with God's help hope a continuation
> or restoration of success. In the events which have brought
> me here I recognise the hand of providence, but nevertheless
> have felt and feel an unfitness which led me at first to try
> to decline the offer made me and now does not yet allow my
> spirits to rise to the level of the position and its duties.
> But perhaps the things of most promise with God begin with
> weakness and fear [FL 63].

In his reply the old Cardinal was complimentary but a little bleak: "I hope you find at Dublin an opening for work such as you desire and which suits you" (FL 413). He would have recalled how, thirty years before, he had been appointed rector of that same institution, then the Catholic University of Ireland, but had fallen into irreconcilable disagreements with the Irish bishops, whose narrowly sectarian ideas of what higher education should be was greatly at odds with his own. Newman had to leave Dublin with little of what he had hoped for accomplished, though his ideals have been preserved in a luminous classic of nineteenth-century thought, *The Idea of a University*. After Newman left, the institution declined, and the buildings, as Hopkins told him, became sadly dilapidated. For many years the college was an object of contention between the British government, which did not want to support a sectarian university, and the Irish bishops, who would accept nothing else. Eventually an elaborate compromise was worked out whereby the college was federated, with other institutions at Galway, Cork and Belfast, into what was known as the Royal University of Ireland. This, however, was, in Matthew Arnold's phrase, "the grand name without the grand thing," for the Royal University was no more than an examining and degree-giving body. The restored University College was placed in the hands of the Jesuits, and when Hopkins arrived it still bore the signs of years of neglect. The original library had been removed to the Diocesan Seminary at Clonliffe; more than four years after Hopkins arrived the books were still there, despite many requests for their return; Hopkins gave a sardonic account of the affair in a letter to Father Ignatius Ryder on 14th November 1888 (FL 64). There was, however, some compensation in congenial colleagues. From the beginning Hopkins greatly admired the Rector, Father Delaney, who "has such a buoyant and unshaken trust in God and wholly lives for the success of the place. He is as generous, cheering and open-hearted a man as ever I lived with" (FL 164). Hopkins found a particular friend in Robert Curtis, Professor of Natural Science, with whom he spent a memorable holiday in North Wales in 1886. Among the better-known members of the faculty was the Professor of English, Thomas Arnold, junior, the brother of Matthew Arnold, and a survivor of Newman's original foundation in 1854. After converting to Catholicism, Arnold had reverted to Anglicanism for a period of several years. His tormenting religious uncertainties were finally resolved when he returned to the Catholic Church, just in time to prevent his election to the chair of Anglo-Saxon at Oxford. When University College was restored, Arnold went back, after thirty years, to his old post. Although in every way overshadowed by his illustrious brother, Thomas Arnold wrote a number of useful books that helped lay the foundation of English studies as an academic discipline. His standard work was *A Manual of English Literature, Historical and Critical,* and Hopkins obliged both Arnold and Canon Dixon by writing a short note on Dixon's poetry for a new edition. It remains Hopkins's one published piece of literary criticism (LD 177).[1]

Hopkins's duties as Professor of Greek fell under the two headings of examining and lecturing. The first of these was a crushing burden; several times a year he had to mark batches of examination papers, up to five hundred at a time, sent in from the constituent colleges of the Royal University. It seems to have been part of the professor's ordinary duties to carry this load single-handed, though nowadays it would be regarded as far too heavy for one man. Even someone of robust health and serene temperament would have been ground down under such a system; Hopkins's delicate health deteriorated further and he felt, at times, close to madness. Examining made demands not only on his stamina but also on his always exigent scrupulosity. One account, written long after his death and perhaps more impressionistically vivid than precisely true, claims that:

[1] It is perhaps worth noting that Thomas Arnold's daughter was the famous novelist, Mrs. Humphry Ward, whose best-known work was *Robert Elsmere* (1888). Among its characters are two Oxford dons, Mr. Langham and Mr. Gray, who are rival mentors to the eponymous hero as an undergraduate. They are fictional portraits of Hopkins's two most distinguished tutors, Walter Pater and T. H. Green. But Robert Elsmere's religious development was in a very different direction from Hopkins's.

As an examiner he caused chaos by indecision in deciding single marks out of possible thousands. He marked each sentence down to halfs and quarters with unerring taste, but his mathematical powers were unfortunately not always equal to adding up the fractions. While the Examining Board were crying for his returns, he would be found with a wet towel round his head agonizing over the delicacy of one mark.[2]

Laments about examining recur throughout the correspondence of Hopkins's last few years. In October 1886 he tells Bridges that, despite the recuperative effects of his recent holiday in Wales, "331 accounts of the First Punic War with trimmings, have sweated me down to nearer my lees and usual alluvial low water mudflats, groans, despair, and yearnings" (LB 236). Lecturing, at first, seemed a lesser evil: "I lecture also and like it well enough, that is rather than not" (FL 164). But in time that became a great burden, too; in March 1889, not long before his death, he wrote to his brother Lionel: "As a tooth ceases aching so will my lectures intermit after tomorrow for Shrovetide" (FL 193). As a lecturer Hopkins seems to have been no great success; as when preaching, he had difficulty in sensing his listeners' needs and interests, and probably talked over their heads much of the time. Indeed, his inveterate scrupulosity made matters even harder than they might have been. As an examiner for the Royal University and a lecturer at University College he was in a slightly anomalous dual role. Objections were made that the students at University College would be in a more advantageous position than students at the other colleges if their lecturer was also the examiner. Hopkins met the difficulty in an uncompromising way by refusing to lecture on anything that was likely to be set in examinations. There was a quixotically idealistic quality about this "solution," which might, indeed, have been admirable if he had been addressing an audience whose only concern was disinterested intellectual enquiry. But his Dublin students, like the generality of

[2] Margaret Bottrall, ed., *Gerard Manley Hopkins: Poems. A Casebook* (London: 1975), p. 63.

students then and now, probably regarded lectures as essential input for examinations. A contributor to the official history of University College refers to Hopkins's inability to communicate very much in his lectures, despite his learning and intellectual subtlety:

> The raw young students who attended his classes in Dublin were little accustomed to such fine distinctions, and there is a legend—true or false, I do not know—that on one famous day they persuaded their professor to lie on the floor and let them drag him round the table by his heels so as to illustrate Hector's fate at Troy.[3]

The poet Katharine Tynan, who knew Hopkins slightly in Dublin, has left a further anecdote about his difficulties with his students:

> He was an English Conservative of the old-fashioned sort and they ragged him. With his strange innocent seriousness he would have invited ragging, though I don't like to think of it as a manifestation of Irish patriotism. Apparently he held his classes in an uproar.
>
> "I do not object to their being rude to me personally," he said, "but I do object to their being rude to their professor and a priest."
>
> It would have been too fine a point for the young barbarians, but Ireland in its political manifestations can be strangely intolerant and intolerable.[4]

To give a balanced picture, one must remark that Hopkins's academic life did not consist entirely of unbroken sessions on the treadmill of examining or riots in the classroom. My impression is that between the dreaded waves of examining and lecturing he had quite a lot of free time, which he filled as well as his poor health and intermittent nervous depression permitted. Most of his time was spent on ambitious scholarly

[3] Michael Tierney, ed., *Struggle with Fortune* (Dublin: 1954), pp. 32–33.
[4] Katharine Tynan, *Memories* (London: 1924), p. 157.

and intellectual schemes, none of which came to anything, and in the composition of music, which he took with great seriousness. Writing poetry was, in comparison, very much an occasional and marginal activity. He had generous vacations, which enabled him to spend time with his family and friends in England, and to enjoy holidays in Wales and Scotland. His life was also much helped by an elderly lady called Miss Cassidy, at whose house in Monasterevan, Kildare, he often stayed; indeed, not long before his death Hopkins wrote that Miss Cassidy "by the change and holiday her kind hospitality provides is become one of the props and struts of my existence" (LB 305).

A history of the Jesuits' connection with University College notes that Hopkins "suffered more or less continuously from nervous depression, and . . . died at a comparatively early age, having been more learned than practical." After paying tribute to his formidable intellectual ability, the account continues dryly: "Some of his pupils appreciated his powers and took advantage of his scholarly teaching; but on the whole he was not happy either in the College work or in the drudgery of the examinations for which he was not well fitted" (LB 319). There is a more qualified but perhaps more expressive account of Hopkins's academic career in a letter that Dixon sent to Bridges in 1893 following a visit to Dublin, when he met and talked to one of the Jesuits who had known Hopkins well:

He, Father Cormac, had a great opinion of Gerard, without, I think, knowing of his genius. He spoke of him as a most delightful companion, & as excellent in his calling, and so on, intimating at the same time that there was something unusual about him; that he was fond of pursuing niceties to an extent that rather stood in the way of his general usefulness. As that he dwelt on the niceties of the language, in his classical lectures, in a way that rather stopped the progress of the classes. Also he was fond of taking up unusual subjects for himself. . . .[5]

[5] James Sambrook, *A Poet Hidden* (London: 1962), pp. 96–97.

On his part, Hopkins had increasing doubts about the value of the college's work. In 1888 he told his mother: "The college is very moderately successful, rather a failure than a success, and there is less prospect of success now than before" (FL 185). Certainly, University College, Dublin, was not at that time a place of great intellectual distinction; particularly not in comparison with the ancient Protestant Anglo-Irish foundation of Trinity College, only half-a-mile away, but separated by gulfs of history and culture. Yet by 1900 University College had been associated with three great writers: the first was Newman; the second was Hopkins himself; and the third was James Joyce, who was two years old when Hopkins arrived in Dublin and who entered the college in 1898.

Despite differences of religion, Hopkins made a few friends at Trinity College. He liked and admired the Professor of Greek, Robert Tyrrell, one of the leading classical scholars of the day, and he had his musical compositions vetted by the Professor of Music, Sir Robert Stewart. One of Stewart's letters refers tartly to Hopkins's endless capacity for explaining and justifying his procedures, however unorthodox and eccentric: "Indeed my dear Padre I *cannot* follow you through your maze of words in your letter of last week. I saw, ere we had conversed ten minutes on our first meeting, that you are one of those special pleaders who never believe yourself wrong in any respect" (FL 427). Eventually, though, Hopkins accepted Stewart's corrections, and was gratified when at length Stewart gave qualified praise to his setting of a lyric by Patmore.

One Trinity man whom Hopkins never met, though he might easily have, was the Professor of English, Edward Dowden, a more distinguished and sophisticated critic and scholar than Thomas Arnold at University College. Hopkins did, however, send Dowden two volumes of Bridges's poetry, as Dowden some years later explained:

We were strangers to each other, and might have been friends. I took for granted that he belonged to the other camp in Irish politics. . . . Father Hopkins was a lover of literature and himself a poet. Perhaps he did in many quarters missionary work on behalf of the poetry of his favourite, Robert Bridges. He certainly left, a good many years since, at my door two volumes by Mr. Bridges, and with them a note begging that I would make no acknowledgement of the gift. I did not acknowledge it then; but with sorrow for a fine spirit lost, I acknowledge it now (LB 248*n*).

Dowden, who was a man of conservative tastes, might not have made much of Hopkins's poems. Nevertheless, he could have provided Hopkins with the intellectual companionship and the opportunity for literary discussion that he so lacked in Dublin. Dowden was an Anglo-Irishman and a Unionist, while Hopkins, though a very reluctant believer in Home Rule, detested Irish nationalism and preferred the company of Unionists. Hence his lonely and alienated position in Dublin. His Catholicism separated him from the Protestants, while his opposition to nationalism separated him from the majority of Catholics, and in particular from the intellectuals and writers, both Catholic and Protestant, of the burgeoning Irish cultural revival. He did, however, know and like one of them, Katharine Tynan, who was just beginning a career as a prolific poet and novelist and supporter of Irish causes. Years later she recalled him as "small and childish-looking, yet like a child-sage, nervous too and very sensitive, with a small ivory-pale face."[6] Hopkins also knew the painter John Butler Yeats, whose studio was in St. Stephen's Green, not far from University College. Indeed, it was there he first met Miss Tynan. There, too, he was given a copy of the first poetic work by William Butler Yeats, reprinted from a Trinity College magazine. As Hopkins told Patmore:

he presented me with *Mosada: a Dramatic Poem* by W. B. Yeats, with a portrait of the author by J. B. Yeats, himself; the young man having finely cut intellectual features and his father being a fine draughtsman. For a young man's pamphlet this was something too much; but you will understand a father's feeling. Now this *Mosada* I cannot think highly of,

[6] Tynan, *op. cit.*, p. 32.

but I was happily not required then to praise what presumably I had not read, and I had read and could praise another piece [FL 373–74].

Towards the end of his life Yeats wrote of Hopkins: "Fifty-odd years ago I met him in my father's studio on different occasions, but remember almost nothing. A boy of seventeen, Walt Whitman in his pocket, had little interest in a querulous, sensitive scholar."[7] When Yeats wrote this the habit of mythologizing his past had taken the place of accurate recollection; he certainly made himself several years too young, for he would have been twenty-one at the time. In earlier years, though, he had preserved a more precise memory of Hopkins. In 1897 he wrote to Robert Bridges: "My first reading of your work was in a book lent me by Prof. Dowden a great many years ago. *Prometheus the Firegiver* it was. I remember talking about it with your friend Father Hopkins and discussing your metrical theories."[8] So much for the brief and unremarked encounter of the two poets who were one day to occupy the first and second place in *The Faber Book of Modern Verse* and other anthologies.

In 1885 Hopkins's depression and spiritual desolation reached a new pitch of crisis. He later described it to Bridges as a state "when my spirits were so crushed that madness seemed to be making approaches—and nobody was to blame, except myself partly for not managing myself better and contriving a change" (LB 222). One result of this crisis was to make Hopkins start writing poetry again after two years of silence. In May he told Bridges he had written two sonnets: "if ever anything was written in blood one of these was" (LB 219). This, according to Bridges, was "Carrion Comfort." By September Hopkins told Bridges that he had "five or more" sonnets ready to send him. These poems cannot be identified with absolute certainty, but it is most probable that they comprise the group known as the "terrible sonnets," Nos. 64 to 69 in the fourth edition of Hop-

[7] W. B. Yeats, ed., *The Oxford Book of Modern Verse* (Oxford: 1936), p. v.

[8] Alan Wade, ed., *The Letters of W. B. Yeats* (London: 1954), p. 281.

kins's *Poems*. In addition to "Carrion Comfort" there is "No worst, there is none," "To seem the stranger lies my lot," "I wake and feel the fell of dark," "Patience, hard thing!" and "My own heart let me more have pity on." These great and famous poems have a critical interest far beyond their autobiographical significance. Nevertheless, they can, in the first instance, be seen as expressions both of Hopkins's crisis and of his efforts to surmount it. Language is strained and stressed almost to breaking-point in enacting this struggle. The poems face despair but without ever wholly succumbing to it; there is a saving energy in them which we do not find in the complaints of weakness and lassitude in Hopkins's letters, and which is in contrast to the outcries of *fin de siècle* despair emerging in the literary culture of the time. Christian readers will see in these poems an expression of a very traditional theme in spiritual writing: the soul's sense of being rejected and left desolate by God. But the poems also, on another level, indicate a remarkable intensity of self-knowledge and self-encounter:

> My own heart let me more have pity on; let
> Me live to my sad self hereafter kind,
> Charitable; not live this tormented mind
> With this tormented mind tormenting yet.

The struggle was never lost and never completely won; it endured. And even in that black year Hopkins could still find solace, however fleeting, in the beauty of nature; as in the fragment that Bridges called "Ashboughs":

> Not of all my eyes see, wandering on the world,
> Is anything a milk to the mind so, so sighs deep
> Poetry to it, as a tree whose boughs break in the sky.

One major element in the crisis of 1885 was Hopkins's deepening sense of isolation in Dublin; this was more than just a matter of an uncongenial environment (though it was partly that, for Hopkins found Dublin's celebrated charm quite resistible) nor of dreary and unfulfilling work. More profoundly, it was a question of Hopkins's sense of identity. In

March he told his mother: "the grief of mind I go through over politics, over what I read and hear and see in Ireland about Ireland and about England is such that I can neither express it nor bear to speak of it" (FL 170). But he did express something of it in one of the sonnets he wrote later in the year:

> To seem the stranger lies my lot, my life
> Among strangers. Father and mother dear,
> Brothers and sisters are in Christ not near
> and he my peace/ my parting, sword and strife.
>
> England, whose honour O all my heart woos, wife
> To my creating thought, would neither hear
> Me, were I pleading, plead nor do I: I wear-
> y of idle a being but by where wars are rife.
>
> I am in Ireland now; now I am at a third
> Remove. Not but in all removes I can
> Kind love both give and get. Only what word
>
> Wisest my heart breeds dark heaven's baffling ban
> Bars or hell's spell thwarts. This to hoard unheard,
> Heard unheeded, leaves me a lonely began.

Hopkins laments, first, his separation from his family in matters of religion, and, secondly, his physical separation from England. The "third remove" is less certain, but I believe that it refers to Hopkins's alienation from the Catholic Church itself in Ireland at that time. The 1880s were, at best, a difficult time for an Englishman in Ireland. There was growing agitation for Home Rule, bitter conflicts between landowners and tenants, boycotts and occasional political murders. Protestants, with a few notable exceptions, were Unionists, and an English Protestant would naturally have inclined to the Unionist cause; he might have found the Irish atmosphere disagreeable, but he would have known where his allegiance lay. For Hopkins the situation was much less straightforward. In England, as a Jesuit, he would have encountered suspicion, perhaps hostility, for there was still widespread prejudice against the Society, long regarded as sinister and un-English. Yet the English Jesuits themselves had no doubt about their English identity, which they traced back to Campion and Southwell and the other Jesuit martyrs of Elizabethan times who had died to defend the traditional faith of Englishmen. This identity was actually strengthened during the centuries of exile in France and Flanders. In England Hopkins felt no more conflict between his faith and his patriotism than Campion or Southwell had.

But in Ireland the leaders of the Catholic Church were Irish patriots. Though they condemned violence and illegality, the bishops were supporters of the nationalist cause; in 1887 Hopkins remarked bitterly: "One archbishop backs robbery, the other rebellion; the people in good faith believe and will follow them" (LB 252). He took some comfort from the fact that the Pope, preferring existing authority to dissidence among small, remote Catholic nations, supported the British government rather than the Irish archbishops. But Cardinal Newman, who had experienced much disappointment in Ireland, was not wholly sympathetic when Hopkins complained to him about the condition of that country. In his reply Newman wrote:

There is one consideration however which you omit. The Irish Patriots hold that they never have yielded themselves to the sway of England and therefore have never been under her laws, and have never been rebels. This does not diminish the force of your picture, but it suggests that there is no help, no remedy. If I were an Irishman, I should be (in heart) a rebel. Moreover, to clench the difficulty the Irish character and tastes are very different from the English [FL 413–14].

Hopkins made an effort to be fair in his understanding of the Irish problem. He acknowledged that the Queen had neglected Ireland and that the Irish owed the royal family little gratitude. Indeed, he admitted that in the past much wrong had been done to Ireland by England but insisted—against the prevalent Irish opinion—that by the 1880s the wrongs had for the most part been put right. In fact, whilst detesting the nationalist movement, Hopkins supported Home Rule, partly because he believed it to be just, and partly because of the disorders that would arise if it were not granted. But he did not believe that any positive good would come from it, and he abhorred the methods used to advance the cause. Hopkins regarded the Irish as an ungovernable people who would never be satisfied. He expressed his sense of alienation in a cold but striking image in a letter written to his mother on Christmas Day 1887. He describes how that morning he had helped to give communion in the church at Monasterevan: "Many hundreds came to the rail, with the unfailing devotion of the Irish; whose religion hangs suspended over their politics as the blue sky over the earth, both in one landscape but immeasurably remote and without contact or interference" (FL 183). It still seems a pertinent observation.

Despite Newman's different view of the question, Hopkins remained convinced that the Catholic Church in Ireland was conniving in rebellion against lawful authority. Such action was alien to the traditions of the Society of Jesus. The Jesuit martyrs of the sixteenth century remained firm in their loyalty to Queen Elizabeth right up to the moment of their execution by the Queen's servants. Furthermore, as part of his theological training Hopkins would have studied the Scholastic theory of the state and the nature of authority; this theory, which had developed long before national sentiment became a factor in politics, could hardly justify the kind of subversion in progress in Ireland. In some moving retreat notes written in January 1889 Hopkins considered his situation in life and what he had made of it. He noted the obstacles to progress, both within his own nature and external to himself; of the latter he wrote:

> Meantime the Catholic Church in Ireland and the Irish Province in it and our College in that are greatly given over to a partly unlawful cause, promoted by partly unlawful means, and against my will my pains, laborious and distasteful, like prisoners made to serve the enemies' gunners, go to help on this cause [SD 262].

In this situation politics was not just an external distraction but something that entered into the heart of Hopkins's anguish.

Casual remarks in his letters during the Dublin years reflect his political bitterness. Like many English Conservatives he had an obsessive loathing of the Liberal Prime Minister, Mr. Gladstone, who had returned to power in 1880. Gladstone was conventionally known as the Grand Old Man, but in Hopkins's correspondence he is called the Grand Old Mischief-Maker and even the Grand Old Traitor. In the middle of a critical discussion of Bridges's play *Nero* Hopkins inserts an abrupt footnote: "there is no depth of stupidity and gape a race could not fall to on the stage that in real life gapes on while Gladstone negotiates his surrenders of the empire" (LB 210). Hopkins knew well enough that such vehement outbursts were lacking in Christian charity and he tried, with imperfect success, to check them. In spiritual notes made in 1888 he wrote: "Let him that is without sin etc—Pray to keep to this spirit and as far as possible rule in speaking of Mr. Gladstone for instance" (SD 260).

Hopkins had always been, as he once told Bridges, "a very great patriot." In reaction to the hostile atmosphere of Dublin his patriotism became strident and even jingoistic. This is apparent in one of his stranger compositions ("the patriotic song for soldiers," as Hopkins called it), "What shall I do for the land that bred me," set to his own musical accompaniment. This song expresses a simplified version of the feeling that inspired his sonnet, "The Soldier." He had innocently admired the military life ever since his few months of serving Cowley Barracks near Oxford. It is an aspect of Hopkins's work and thought that now seems remote. More interesting, and more rewarding, is the strain of assertive pride in the achievements of English culture that Hopkins came to show, perhaps as a deliberate reaction against the prevailing spirit of Irish and Celtic cultural nationalism. In 1886 he defends Wordsworth's "Immortality Ode" against criticisms by Canon Dixon, in a pleasing image that draws together Hopkins's patriotism, his religion and his love of English poetry: "For my part I shd. think St. George and St. Thomas of Canterbury wore roses in heaven for England's sake on the day that ode, not without their intercession, was penned . . ." (LD 148). At about the same time he tells Bridges that true poets should seek fame, not just for their own sake but for their country's:

A great work by an Englishman is like a great battle won by England. It is an unfading bay tree. It will even be admired by and praised by and do good to those who hate England (as England is most perilously hated), who do not wish even to be benefited by her [LB 231].

Hopkins's fullest exposition of his cultural nationalism occurs in a letter to Patmore dated 4th June 1886. He first tells his friend: "Your poems are a good deed done for the Catholic Church and another for England, for the British Empire, which now trembles in the balance held in the hand of unwisdom." He then goes on to develop his ideal of Empire which, like most Victorians, he saw not as a means of exploitation but of spreading freedom, law and civilization: "Then there is civilization. It should have been Catholic truth. That is the great end of Empires before God, to be Catholic and draw nations into their Catholicism. But our Empire is less and less Christian as it grows." There seems to be a millennial hint here that, following the still hoped-for and prayed-for conversion of England, a Holy British Empire might be the means of bringing the Catholic faith to the whole world. Hopkins continues with some searching reflections on the nature of English civilization, in which there was clearly so much wrong, and wonders what positive qualities it might still have to offer the world:

what marked and striking excellence has England to shew to make her civilization attractive? Her literature is one of her excellences and attractions and I believe that criticism will tend to make this more and more felt; but there must be more of that literature, a continued supply and in quality excellent [FL 367–68].

This, at least, is a sentiment that the present-day English reader may share, however dated Hopkins's other expressions of patriotic and imperialistic fervour may now appear. What he does not acknowledge, though, is that the English language and literature in English—as distinguished from English literature—extend far beyond England, or even the United Kingdom. I now return the account to the summer of 1885. By August

Hopkins had somewhat recovered from his mental and spiritual crisis, perhaps helped by writing the poems it produced. He returned to England for a holiday with his family, at Hampstead and then at Midhurst in Sussex. He concluded the visit with a few days as the guest of Patmore at Hastings. Patmore continued to have the highest opinion of Hopkins as a critic, and incorporated many of his suggestions into the new edition of *The Angel in the House*. He had, however, quite failed to appreciate Hopkins's poems, much to his embarrassment. (Patmore told Bridges: "To me his poetry has the effect of veins of pure gold imbedded in masses of unpracticable quartz" [FL 353n].) At Hastings Hopkins was made thoroughly at home by Patmore's young third wife, Harriet. He was impressed with the artistic talents of Patmore's daughter, Bertha, and noted with concerned interest the unusually refined sensibility and imagination of his youngest child, the two-and-a-half-year-old Francis Epiphanius, known as "Piffy." "I should not like it in a brother of mine," Hopkins told his mother, in an unexpected flash of Broad Church briskness.

During this visit Hopkins read the manuscript of a short prose work by Patmore called *Sponsa Dei*, an incident which was to have a disconcerting sequel. Patmore's dominant theme as a poet was love, both human and divine, and his exploration of it took some strange and idiosyncratic forms. He was a devout but individualistic Catholic, keenly interested in mystical experience; at the same time, his library contained a sizeable collection of erotic literature. Some of the odes in *The Unknown Eros* present the love of man for woman as an image of Christ's love for the soul. It was a traditional theme in mystical theology, deriving ultimately from the Song of Songs, and was given vivid expression in works of Baroque art, like Bernini's statue of St. Teresa in ecstasy and the poetry of Marino and Crashaw. In *The Unknown Eros* Patmore treats the subject with a remarkably intense eroticism that made few concessions to Victorian religious conventions and sensibility. *Sponsa Dei* was, it seems, a more extended treatment in prose of the dual theme of divine and sexual love, and was the fruit of many years' reflection. It is evident that Hopkins did not like parts of *Sponsa Dei* when he read it, though we can only conjecture about his reaction. It is probable, though, that Hopkins felt Patmore had gone dangerously far in his association of the two modes of love; what might have been acceptable in the poetic language and allegorical disguise of *The Unknown Eros* might have appeared scandalous in a direct and extended treatment in prose. But there is no reason to suppose that Hopkins objected to the whole work. In a letter of thanks to Patmore, written after his return to Dublin on 21st August, Hopkins remarked: "I am glad you let me read the autobiographical tract: it will be a valuable testimony." (I am assuming that he is here referring to *Sponsa Dei*, rather than to the autobiographical fragment that Patmore wrote some years later.) Hopkins then adds a rather allusive and embarrassed but still fairly explicit paragraph about the possible abuses of mystical contemplation (FL 365). He evidently has in mind the way in which some heterodox contemplatives have engaged in sexual activity under the conviction that they were free from any trace of sin in doing so; it is a well-known topic in the pathology of mysticism, though perhaps less familiar then than now. Patmore took these comments seriously, as he did all Hopkins's judgments on his work, but responded with a curious combination of inactivity and impulsiveness. For well over two years he did nothing; then, on Christmas Day 1887, he burnt the manuscript. He later told Hopkins: "Much-meditating on the effect which my M.S. 'Sponsa Dei' had upon you, when you read it while staying here, I concluded that I would not take the responsibility of being the first to expound the truths contained therein . . ." (FL 385). Hopkins was surprised and disconcerted at the news. He believed that Patmore had taken a needlessly severe and final step and that nothing in his own judgment on *Sponsa Dei* had warranted it:

> My objections were not final, they were but considerations (I forget now, with one exception, what they were); even if they were valid, still if you had kept to yr. custom of consulting your director [Patmore's confessor and spiritual director], as you said you should, the book might have ap-

peared with no change or with slight ones. But now regret
is useless [FL 385–86].

Certainly Patmore seems to have had no regrets or second
thoughts about the act of destruction, but even, in fact, to have
been rather proud of it. Writing to Bridges after Hopkins's
death, he presented the incident as a sign of his respect for
Hopkins's judgment:

> The *authority* of his goodness was so great with me that
> I threw the manuscript of a little book—a sort of "Religio
> Poetae"—into the fire, simply because, when he read it, he
> said with a grave look, "that's telling secrets." This little
> book had been the work of ten years' continual meditations,
> and could not but have made a greater effect than all the
> rest I have ever written; but his doubt was final with me
> [FL 391].

One would not guess from this account that so much time
elapsed before Patmore burnt the manuscript; he seems to be
mythologizing the episode and the memory of his dead friend
with Yeatsian fervour. The facts remain obscure, but enough
is known to exculpate Hopkins from the charge laid by Edmund
Gosse of meddling in Patmore's affairs to the extent of pro-
voking so wanton an act of literary vandalism. *Sponsa Dei*
may have been, as Gosse called it, a "vanished masterpiece,"
but another friend of Patmore's, Frederick Greenwood, also had
doubts about the wisdom of publishing it; indeed, long after
Patmore's death he wrote: "I have never regretted counselling
suppression." As a final word one may add that Patmore's
close friend Alice Meynell believed that much of the contents
of *Sponsa Dei* reappeared in his last book of essays, *The Rod,
the Root, and the Flower.*

Hopkins never saw Patmore again though they kept up their
correspondence. He was, however, in England for a further
vacation in the spring of 1886 and took the opportunity of
visiting, for the first time, Bridges's country house at Yattendon
in Berkshire and met the lady whom Bridges had married when
he was forty. After a second and longer visit the following

year he told Bridges: "I had the impression I had never in my life met a sweeter lady than Mrs. Bridges. You may wear a diamond on your finger and yet never have seen it in a side light, so I tell you" (LB 263–64). In May 1887 Hopkins visited the Royal Academy, for the first time in several years. He and Dixon, who had also been there, later exchanged notes about it. They also discussed an exhibition of Whistler's paintings then on in London. Dixon, true to his developing post-Victorian taste, found Whistler "a man of great genius," if eccentric and puzzling, who had been done a great injustice by Ruskin. Hopkins was in cautious agreement:

> I agree to Whistler's striking genius—feeling for what I call *inscape* (the very soul of art); but then his execution is so negligible, unpardonably so sometimes (that was, I suppose, what Ruskin particularly meant by "throwing the pot of paint in the face of the public"): *his* genius certainly has not come to puberty [LD 135].

As far as he could Hopkins kept up his interest in painting, and sent his brothers Arthur and Everard, both professional artists, detailed and quite sharp criticisms of their work. In 1888 he himself took to sketching again, after an interval of many years, and became interested in photography.

Hopkins took up new subjects and tried to extend his existing interests more and more in the Dublin years. There is an undeniable impression of dilettantism and dissipation of energy, though Hopkins believed that his scholarly enquiries would eventually produce new and important advances in knowledge. Early in 1886 he was still trying to get on with the book on Homer's art that he had started at Stonyhurst. Then he began a long and detailed correspondence with Alexander Baillie, who was an authority on Egyptian matters, about the possible Egyptian origins of Greek civilization. This involved a rapid sequence of letters and closely-written postcards full of abstruse and energetic speculations on questions of etymology and comparative mythology. The discussion shows that Hopkins was a very learned man and, furthermore, that he was not afraid to guess boldly about what he did not know. It also suggests that he was, at one and the same time, something of a crank and very aware of the central intellectual movements of his age. I am reminded both of George Eliot's Mr. Casaubon, amateurishly seeking the "key to all mythologies," and of Sir James Frazer's systematic enquiry into the myths of mankind, then in progress, which culminated in the first volume of *The Golden Bough* in 1890. Hopkins found an intense intellectual excitement in these speculations; quite literally, they took his mind off his troubles. He concludes one letter by telling Baillie:

> It is a great help to me to have someone interested in something (that will answer my letters), and it supplies some sort of intellectual stimulus. I sadly need that and a general stimulus to being, so dull and yet harassed is my life [FL 263].

But by the end of 1886 he is moving on to a new interest, or perhaps reviving an earlier one. He tells Baillie: "Egypt is off with me just now and very serious work touching Pindar and the theory of rhythm and the 'Dorian Measure' is on, but I cannot do what I would for want of mathematics" (FL 275). Despite his lack of mathematical ability Hopkins persisted with the project for some months. At first the intention, though ambitious, was fairly well defined; Hopkins believed that in the Dorian Measure he would find "the true scansion of perhaps half or more than half of the Greek and Latin lyric verse: I do believe it is a great and it is an unsuspected discovery" (FL 374). A few weeks later the scheme had grown: "my purpose is, in explaining the Dorian Measure, to bring in the most fundamental principles of art, to write almost a philosophy of art and illustrate that by the Dorian Measure" (LB 247). In January 1887 Hopkins tells Patmore that he is to present his ideas in a paper delivered to a physical and mathematical science club which met once a month at the Royal Dublin Society:

> Writing it has naturally cleared my mind and indeed opened out a sort of new world. I believe that I can now set music

and metre both of them on a scientific footing which will be final like the law of gravitation. This is a great boast, God grant it may not be an empty one [FL 377].

The paper grew into a book. On 1st May Hopkins told Bridges: "I have written a good deal of my book on the Dorian Measure or on Rhythm in general. Indeed it is on almost everything elementary and is much of it physics and metaphysics. It is full of new words, without which there can be no new science" (LB 254). On 12th May Hopkins gave a further account of it to Patmore. After saying, "For the purpose of grounding the matter thoroughly I am subjecting the terms of geometry, line, surface, and solid and so on, many others to a searching examination. Most therefore of what I have written is metaphysics and stiff reading . . . ," he goes on to say that the work will have to be rewritten in time, and then concludes ominously: "Still I have great doubts whether I shall be able to get on. It can only be done in spare time, and what is far harder, spare strength, so to speak" (FL 379). Nothing now remains of this wildly ambitious and, doubtless, impractical proposal, where the Mr. Casaubon side of Hopkins's nature seems to have been well to the fore. By December 1887 he is once more engaged in writing music: "I am at work on a great choral fugue! I can hardly believe it," he told Dixon (LD 154).

Nor was that all. Other surprising notions would be suddenly picked up and just as suddenly dropped. Thus, in August 1886, when his Egyptian interests were waning and before the onset of his obsession with the Dorian Measure, and when he had just been marking examination papers for several weeks on end, Hopkins told Dixon that he was writing "a sort of popular account of Light and the Ether" (LD 139), though he acknowledged in the very next sentence that it would not really be popular nor indeed easy reading. No more is heard of that. But two years later Hopkins announced that he had written a paper on an equally unlikely subject, "Statistics and Free Will," which, again, has not survived. One has the distinct and disconcerting impression of a powerful, original and well-stocked—indeed, polymathic—mind with so little equilibrium that it could not resist picking up and trying to pursue one random proposal after another. No doubt from Hopkins's own point of view everything, potentially at least, hung together; leaving aside the odd flirtation with scientific topics, one can see how this might be so. Hopkins's interest in language, in the theory of metre and music, and his practical efforts in composing music and writing poetry, might one day all converge in a great intellectual and aesthetic structure. One can quote the graphic but baffled recollection of Father Clement Barraud, set down thirty years after Hopkins's death:

> I once wrote to my friend from Demerara, describing the Feast of Lanterns, as celebrated there by the resident Chinese. His reply was a learned disquisition on Chinese music, God save the mark! discussing its peculiar tonality, and claiming for it merits which had certainly escaped my observation.[9]

Some remote ideal of unity might have spurred Hopkins on in his fragmentary projects despite his incapacity ever to complete anything. Yet poetry apart, practically nothing remains of all these schemes. Some articles and papers were finished, and Hopkins expected them to appear in such publications as *The Irish Monthly*, *Hermathena* (a review published at Trinity College) and the *Classical Review*. But none was ever published, apart from two unsigned translations of Shakespeare songs into Latin that came out in *The Irish Monthly*. The pattern of editorial rebuff first established by *The Month* continued, but whether this can be blamed entirely on the malignity of fate and the perversity of editors, or whether Hopkins refused, through stubbornness or eccentricity, to present his work in a form suitable for publication, is a matter for speculation. In May 1888 these disappointments evoked from Hopkins the strange and poignant reflection: "to me, to finish a thing and that it shd. be out of hand and owe its failure to somebody else is nearly the same thing as success" (LB 277). Another

---

[9] "C.B.," "Recollections of Father Gerard Hopkins," *The Month*, July 1919.

new activity was collecting Irish words and phrases for an
English Dialect dictionary then in preparation. This, at least,
was much closer to his central interests as a poet than his
more abstruse intellectual schemes, and it did result in tiny
but perceptible recognition. In the first volume of Joseph
Wright's massive *English Dialect Dictionary* there is a list of
Unprinted Collections of Dialect Words quoted in the dictionary; one of the many compilers there named is the "Rev.
G. M. Hopkins, Ireland." So much effort and striving with so
little to show for it led Hopkins to regard himself as "time's
eunuch," a phrase he used in his correspondence and expressed
memorably in one of his last sonnets:

> birds build—but not I build; no, but strain,
> Time's eunuch, and not breed one work that wakes.

In a letter to Dixon Hopkins made a measured statement
about success and failure, with Christ as the great exemplar:

> Above all Christ our Lord: his career was cut short and,
> whereas he would have wished to succeed by success—for
> it is insane to lay yourself out for failure, prudence is the first
> of the cardinal virtues, and he was the most prudent of men—
> nevertheless he was doomed to succeed by failure; his plans
> were baffled, his hopes dashed, and his work was done by
> being broken off undone. However much he understood all
> this he found it an intolerable grief to submit to it. He left
> the example: it is very strengthening, but except in that sense
> it is not consoling [LD 137–38].

Some failure is unavoidable in any human life. But Hopkins
lived with a strong conviction of failure, and, as he was aware
in his more clear-sighted moments, it arose partly from the
perversities of his temperament. He was fatally drawn to
self-defeating courses; and, in small but important matters,
to self-neglect. Thus, in January 1887 he complains to his
mother of eye-strain and says he will have to get glasses. In
September 1888 he tells Bridges that he is suffering from "gout
in the eyes," and only in October 1888 has he finally taken to
wearing glasses.

In the long run, of course, Hopkins did "succeed by failure." The present-day reader, recognising Hopkins as a major English poet, will probably regard the time-consuming and fruitless distractions of his Dublin years with impatience or regret. He did not write many poems in Dublin, but they are among his greatest; perhaps, if he had given less time to other things, he would have written more poetry. But given the complexities of his nature, one has no real reason to suppose this. The composition of the "terrible sonnets" in 1885 does seem to have released a fresh spring of creativeness in Hopkins. But he never discussed his poetry with the same portentousness and excitement that he gave to his scholarly projects and his musical compositions. He refused to devote much time to writing verse, and in some respects regarded it as an inferior form of musical composition. In 1887 he told Patmore: "such verse as I do compose is oral, made away from paper, and I put it down with repugnance" (FL 379). All the completed Dublin poems were written either in conventional Petrarchan sonnet form, or in Hopkins's own variation on it, and such a form is easily memorized. Some idea of his method of composition is indicated in a letter to Dixon of 29th July 1888, where he says: "there was one windy bright day between floods last week; fearing for my eyes, with my other rain of papers, I put work aside and went out for the day, and conceived a sonnet" (LD 157). And in October Hopkins tells Bridges that his sonnet, "St. Alphonsus Rodriguez," was "made out of doors in the Phoenix Park with my mind's eye on the first presentment of the thought" (LB 297). Composing poetry, it seems, was an oral, peripatetic activity, carried on in moments snatched from academic work or study. It is perhaps significant that two of the poems he started at that time, in more extended forms than the sonnet, were left unfinished. One was "On the Portrait of Two Beautiful Young People," inspired by a picture he had seen at Monasteraven in December 1886. Another was an "Epithalamion" for the marriage of his brother Everard in 1888, which Hopkins had to abandon, to his distress and embarrassment, after an elaborate opening.

In December 1887 Hopkins told Dixon:

I enclose two sonnets, works of infinite, of over great contrivance, I am afraid, to the annulling in the end of the right effect. They have also too much resemblance to each other; but they were conceived at the same time. They are of a "robustious" sort and perhaps "Tom's Garland" approaches bluster and will remind you of Mr. Podsnap with his back to the fire. They are meant for, and cannot properly be taken in without, emphatic recitation; which nevertheless is not an easy performance [LD 153].

Here, as elsewhere, Hopkins shows himself as formidable a critic of his own work as of others', for the consensus of critical opinion is precisely that these two sonnets—"Tom's Garland" and "Harry Ploughman"—are over-contrived and that the excess of detail prevents a total effect. Dixon found "Tom's Garland" particularly hard going and wrote to Bridges for a crib, but neither of them could make much of it. Hopkins told Bridges that he had laughed sardonically at their predicament, and he obliged them with an explanation of the poem. There is a somewhat tongue-in-cheek air about this dexterous piece of decoding: "O, once explained, how clear it all is!" Hopkins parenthetically remarks in the middle of it. The explanation is most interesting in its revelation of Hopkins's Tory Radical political stance. He refers to the traditional idea that everyone in society, even the lowliest, should be part of the Commonwealth and share in the common weal, and goes on:

the curse of our times is that many do not share it, that they are outcasts from it and have neither security nor splendour; that they share care with the high and obscurity with the low, but wealth or comfort with neither. And this state of things, I say, is the origin of Loafers, Tramps, Cornerboys, Roughs, Socialists and other pests of society [LB 273–74].

The other poem, "Harry Ploughman," is somewhat similar, inasmuch as it is a study of a working man, but it has a less complicated programme underlying it. Indeed, Hopkins conceived it as a piece of simple descriptive verse. In its appreciation of the ploughman's physique it inevitably raises the question of Hopkins's possible homosexual inclinations; particularly when we recall that Hopkins asked Bridges if there were anything like it in Walt Whitman, saying he hoped not but feared there might be. The first readers of Hopkins's published poetry would, no doubt, have recoiled even from the discussion of such a possibility. Now, however, the pendulum has swung so far the other way that it is often taken for granted that Hopkins was *tout court* a homosexual and that all his psychological problems arose from this one unacknowledged cause. This seems to me crudely reductive, just as the previous attitude now looks unacceptably naive. As I remarked in an earlier chapter, Hopkins grew up at a time when romantic friendships between men, with warm expressions of sentiment, were both common and acceptable. In some cases, one imagines, sexual feelings entered into the relationship, but without being necessarily recognised and accepted as such. Unlike the Victorians, we know that human sexuality is by no means stable and that the male-female division is far from absolute. Yet to assume that all close friendships between men are "really" homosexual, as is often done now, is to succumb to a very simplistic form of Freudianism. In the case of Hopkins I think a degree of open-mindedness, even agnosticism, is necessary. There is, in any event, a logical difficulty in saying what the actual sexual proclivities of a committed celibate might be. If Hopkins had not been a priest and a very scrupulous Christian, he might have been a practising homosexual; but if one thing is posited as different, other things might have been different too, and he could equally well have been a conventionally heterosexual married man, like his brothers. Or he might have had a somewhat indeterminate sexual nature. On the evidence available to us one can only say that Hopkins was, throughout his life, fascinated by male beauty and made no attempt to disguise this fascination. This can certainly be regarded as denoting a homosexual element in his make-up, which is not the same thing as possessing a homosexual nature (if such a phrase makes any sense). Hopkins himself saw mas-

culine beauty—in a quasi-platonic way—as imperfectly reflecting the supreme beauty of Christ, about which he preached
at Bedford Leigh in 1879:

> I leave it to you, brethren, then to picture him, in whom the
> fulness of the godhead dwelt bodily, in his bearing how
> majestic, how strong and yet how lovely and lissome in his
> limbs, in his look how earnest, grave but kind. In his Passion
> all this strength was spent, this lissomness crippled, this
> beauty wracked, this majesty beaten down. But it is now
> more than all restored, and for myself I make no secret I
> look forward with eager desire to seeing the matchless
> beauty of Christ's body in the heavenly light [SD 36].

In my own judgment the real conflict in Hopkins's nature
was not sexual at all, but was between his strong desire for
success and recognition and his equally strong dread of them.
It was this conflict, I believe, that led him into such perverse
and self-defeating courses of behaviour in his practical life. He
was a remarkably wilful man and his will was often at odds
with itself. He saw the hard choices of life not as between
good and evil, but between conflicting forms of good, and was
always very concerned with the nature of choice. In pursuing
this interest Hopkins developed a Scotist distinction between
the "elective will" and the "affective will," which is, in every-
day language, something like the distinction between desire and
choice. In the opinion of Father Devlin, Hopkins exaggerated
and over-dramatized the division between them (SD 116ff).

In August 1888 Hopkins crossed the Irish Sea for the last
time. After six weeks of examining he spent a fortnight's
holiday in the Highlands with his friend Robert Curtis. He
told Bridges that in a sermon at Fort William he could put plainly
what he had put not at all plainly to the rest of the world, or
rather to Bridges and Dixon, in a new sonnet in sprung rhythm
with two codas. This was "That Nature is a Heraclitean Fire
and of the comfort of the Resurrection." It is an extraordinary
poem, complicated, certainly, but not in the tortuously contrived
way of "Tom's Garland." Nor is it at all like the conventional

idea of a sonnet. In its opening it returns in spirit to the joyful nature poems of Hopkins's last year in Wales, but the joy is fleeting. Nature is as beautiful as ever in its changing and glittering appearances. Yet underneath all is flux, nothing is stable, and the achievements of man do not endure in the darkness. But in the end the Resurrection sends its "eternal beam" and the poet—and mankind, "This Jack, joke, poor potsherd"—can say: "I am all at once what Christ is, since he was what I am." The assurance is real but has not been easily obtained; behind the hard-won ultimate serenity of this poem one senses the near-despair of the "terrible sonnets." Another poem written that autumn, "St. Alphonsus Rodriguez," is comparatively simple. Indeed, Hopkins insisted to Bridges: "The sonnet (I say it snorting) aims at being intelligible" (RB 293). It commemorates a lay-brother of the Society of Jesus, lately canonized, who had lived a life of total obscurity and great inner sanctity; one can see why the subject appealed to Hopkins. At about this time Hopkins received the disturbing news that one of his closest undergraduate friends, Father William Addis, who had been received into the Catholic Church a few days before Hopkins himself, had abandoned both the priesthood and the Church in order to marry one of his parishioners. (He became successively a Presbyterian minister in Australia, a Unitarian in Oxford and, in the last years of his life, an Anglican clergyman.) Bridges took the opportunity of Addis's defection to indulge in some anti-Catholic sentiment, much to Hopkins's distress and anger. Yet this incident apart, Hopkins's mood in 1888–89 seems to have been calmer and more composed than in his first few years in Dublin. Christopher Devlin has suggested that the retreat notes made by Hopkins in January 1889 point to the difficult resolution of a personal crisis:

> Emotionally, they are unnerving; but intellectually they present the spectacle of a classic ascent according to the rules—though whether he was right to choose so steep a cliff-face is another matter. For three days he gives clear,

trenchant expression to all his lurking griefs—politics, illness, scruples, failures; he explores every crevice unflinch-
ingly, and the result is apparently complete abandonment—
"helpless loathing."

Then on the fifth day is felt the grinding application—
"We hear our hearts grate on themselves"—of Fr. Whitty's
rule, to concentrate on the immediate duties of one's state
[SD 220].

Then follows Hopkins's notes for 5th January:

But I say to myself that I am only too willing to do God's
work and help on the knowledge of the Incarnation. But
this is not really true: I am not willing enough for the piece
of work assigned me, the only work I am given to do, though
I could do others if they were given. This is my work at
Stephen's Green. And I thought that the Royal University
was to me what Augustus's enrolment was to St. Joseph:
exit sermo a Caesare Augusto etc.; so resolution of the
senate of the R.U. came to me, inconvenient and painful,
but the journey to Bethlehem was inconvenient and painful;
and then I am bound in justice, and paid. I hope to bear this
in mind [SD 263].

The last surviving photograph of Hopkins, taken in 1888,
shows him looking remarkably young for a man of forty-four.
Indeed, he had already been teased about his youthful appearance by Katharine Tynan: "She told me that when she first
saw me she took me for 20 and some friend of hers for 15; but
it won't do; they should see my heart and vitals, all shaggy with
the whitest hair" (LB 250). By 1888 his hair, though still dark,
had receded a little, and the cheek-bones were more prominent
than in earlier portraits, but otherwise there was little change:
there was the same strong nose and chin and firmly assertive
mouth. His health remained poor, though. In the spring of 1889
Hopkins was visited by his old Oxford friend Francis de
Paravicini, who found him looking ill and depressed. De
Paravicini was concerned at his friend's condition and resolved

to do something about it, principally by getting Hopkins moved back to England from the uncongenial atmosphere of Dublin. He was a Catholic layman of some influence, and his efforts were about to succeed when Hopkins died.

Perhaps because of de Paravicini's visit and promise of help Hopkins's spirits were lightened. On 29th April he wrote to Bridges: "I am ill today, but no matter for that as my spirits are good" (LB 303). With this letter he enclosed a sonnet addressed specifically to Bridges. It is a stark and lucid but not at all despairing acceptance of limitation, the calm and measured utterance of a man "who has come through":

> Sweet fire the sire of muse, my soul needs this;
> I want the one rapture of an inspiration.
> O then if in my lagging lines you miss
>
> The roll, the rise, the carol, the creation,
> My winter world, that scarcely breathes that bliss
> Now, yields you, with some sighs, our explanation.

After the syntactical deformations and the strange diction of some of his earlier poems, this last sonnet has a striking power and simplicity. And much the same thing is true of the other two sonnets written in the spring of 1889 (Nos. 74 and 75 in the Fourth Edition of *Poems*). "Thou art indeed just, Lord" is equally autobiographical; the poet accepts the aridity of his role as "Time's eunuch" and ends with the plea, "Mine, O thou lord of life, send my roots rain." "The shepherd's brow" was found too "cynical" by Bridges to be included in the canon of Hopkins's poems and he relegated it to the drafts and fragments. Yet it is clearly a completed sonnet and deserves its place. "Cynical" is the wrong word for it, though it takes a black view of human feebleness and folly; one finds similar expressions of impatience with human nature in Hopkins's letters. It ends on the note of wry self-deprecation so familiar in the letters:

> And I that die these deaths, that feed this flame,
> That . . . in smooth spoons spy life's masque mirrored: tame
> My tempests there, my fire and fever fussy.

I believe that the poems of Hopkins's last year of life—"That Nature is a Heraclitean Fire," "St. Alphonsus Rodriguez," "Thou art indeed just, Lord," "The shepherd's brow" and "To R.B."—enhance each other, and taken as a group represent both a new artistic maturity and a further stage of Hopkins's spiritual development and self-awareness.

He did not recover from the illness that he had treated so lightly in his letter to Bridges. Two days later he told his mother he thought he was suffering from rheumatic fever—"which comes very inconveniently when I shd. be and am setting my Papers for the examinations"—though he hoped to be better by the next day; if he were not he would see a doctor. By 5th May Hopkins was in bed and under medical care; he had decided it was an ill wind that blows nobody any good and that he would at least enjoy the unexpected relief from university work. By the 8th he was in so weak a state that he could only dictate a letter to his mother, though it is cheerful enough, full of musical and literary allusions. Only then had his illness been finally and correctly diagnosed as typhoid. He lingered on in a weak state for several weeks; at one point Father Wheeler, the Vice President of University College, thought he was improving, but it was a false hope. On 5th June he took a serious turn for the worse and his parents were summoned from England. They were with him when he died on 8th June, at one-thirty in the afternoon, calmly attentive almost to the end to the prayers being said around him. Father G. F. Lahey, Hopkins's first biographer, wrote that his final words were: "I am so happy, I am so happy."[10]

Hopkins was buried in the Jesuits' burial ground at Glasnevin. He was mourned by those who had loved him as a son and brother and friend. He was remembered by a wider circle who had known him under various aspects: a learned if impractical member of the Society of Jesus; a Professor of Greek;

[10] Father Lahey produced no sources for his assertions. If I approach this one with caution, though certainly not with disbelief, it is because it fits a little too neatly certain biographical conventions of the death-bed scene. See Chapter 3, "The Death Scene," in *Truth to Life: The Art of Biography in the Nineteenth Century* by A. O. J. Cockshut (London: 1974).

a brilliant and eccentric scholar; an Englishman unhappy in Ireland; an amateur composer. He was also remembered as a man who, for all his anxiety and self-doubt, was deeply devoted to the priesthood. After his death, Mrs. de Paravicini wrote to Mrs. Hopkins:

> He was so lovable—so singularly gifted—& in his saintliness, so apart from, & different to, all others. Only that his beautifully gentle and generous nature made him one with his friends; & led us to love & to value him,—feeling that our lives were better, & the world richer, because of him. . . . My husband remembers how he would speak of his enjoyment in the saying his Office, & in the quiet completeness of his religion [J 301].

Least of all was Hopkins remembered as a poet, certainly not in Dublin, where he seems to have thoroughly concealed the fact that he wrote poetry. After his death Bridges began his long and careful custodianship of his friend's manuscript poems. Those who knew or were in touch with Bridges, like Edward Dowden, were made to understand that the dead Jesuit had been a poet of great originality and distinction. Under Bridges's sponsorship occasional poems by Hopkins appeared in anthologies, such as *The Poets and Poetry of the Century* in 1893; and *Lyra Sacra* and *A Book of Christmas Verse*, both edited in 1895 by H. C. Beeching, who was related by marriage to Bridges. Some of Hopkins's letters were published in 1900 in the *Memoirs and Correspondence of Coventry Patmore*, and he was mentioned in the introductions to Bridges's editions of poems by Richard Watson Dixon (1909) and Digby Mackworth Dolben (1911). He is referred to in Wilfrid Ward's massive life of Newman as the recipient of a letter from Newman about the Irish problem. Extracts from Hopkins's journals appeared in a Jesuit magazine in 1906 and 1907; and in *The Month*, twenty years after Hopkins's death, Father Keating, S.J., published an affectionate memoir of him. (Father Keating wanted to bring out an edition of Hopkins's poems, but was rebuffed by Bridges.) The establishment of Hopkins's reputation was a slow process but it went on steadily; several poems appeared in anthologies of religious poetry—one of them edited by Katharine Tynan—and in 1912 a poem was included in Sir Arthur Quiller-Couch's *Oxford Book of Victorian Verse;* one is reminded of a phrase from Hopkins's sonnet on St. Alphonsus Rodriguez, "trickling increment." In 1917 Bridges, by then Poet Laureate and a distinguished public figure, edited a much-read anthology, *The Spirit of Man,* in which more of Hopkins's poems appeared and aroused interest. The following year Bridges's slim, handsomely-produced edition of the *Poems* appeared. Hopkins as a poet was at last in the public domain, though it would be another ten years or more before he became widely read and admired. Hopkins had thought it proper for a poet to seek fame, as he frequently told Bridges, Dixon and Patmore, but refused ever to seek it for himself. He was prepared to leave his ultimate reputation in God's hands. In the end recognition came; slowly at first, then abundantly.

6

"Nearly Hard Poems' King"

I

IT WAS A RECENT happy discovery of the poet Roy Fuller that the words "Gerard Manley Hopkins" can be rearranged into the anagram forming the title of this chapter.[1] The discovery might well have pleased Hopkins, who had a Victorian liking for word-play, and who jotted down possible variations on his own name in an early diary (J 48). He was also much given to images of kingship, though if asked who was the actual king of hard poems, he would probably have answered: "Why, Christ Our Lord!" Christ was the king of all his poems, hard or easy, and of everything else in creation.

Hopkins's hardest poem is also his longest, and the first work of his maturity as a poet. Bridges described "The Wreck of the *Deutschland*" as "like a great dragon folded in the gate to forbid all entrance" when he placed it at the beginning of his edition of the poems. In Hopkins's lifetime it defeated the editor of *The Month* and most other readers; a hundred years after its composition the poem has attracted many would-be

---

[1] "Nemo's Page," *The New Review*, No. 14, (London: 1975).

dragon slayers in the form of commentators and explicators, and some of the difficulties have been satisfactorily explained. Yet the poem, taken as a whole, is still bewildering, conveying an effect of confused magnificence. In it Hopkins brings together—perhaps forces together—things that have no necessary connection, beyond their personal urgency for him. The opportunity to write the poem after the self-imposed silence of the previous eight years enabled him to express—in the literal sense, meaning "to squeeze out"—the themes that were moving him in December 1875; some new and public, like the shipwreck, others private and of long standing. The first part of the poem is about a spiritual crisis in Hopkins's life; the second is about the wreck of the ship and the sufferings of the crew and passengers, which Hopkins had seen described in newspaper reports, and which initially inspired him. (In this aspect "The Wreck of the *Deutschland*" is like other famous nineteenth-century works whose origin lay in newspaper stories, such as *Le Rouge et le Noir* and *Crime and Punishment*). Furthermore, the whole poem is a formal and metrical experiment of great ambition and complexity, of a kind that Hopkins had been entertaining for some time. Formally and verbally the poem is more idiosyncratic than anything else by Hopkins. Its structure is based on the Pindaric ode, which permitted a loose, free, almost improvised thematic development. At the same time, the stanza form is strict and exacting: the combination of freedom and strictness was to typify Hopkins's later poetry and lay at the heart of his nature as priest and poet. "The Wreck of the *Deutschland*" was not only the embodiment of Hopkins's "new rhythm," the innovatory metric that he called "sprung rhythm"; it also reflected his interest in the elaborate verbal patterning of Welsh poetry, which he had been studying at St. Beuno's. And in the interests of immediacy and vividness Hopkins employed English syntax with a freedom, even a fluidity, that was far removed from the norms, not just of prose, but of most English verse. Nearly everything about "The Wreck of the *Deutschland*" is difficult. Its subject matter is remote from the modern reader, who is likely to know little about religious experience, and is scarcely more familiar with shipwrecks. Its form can still seem overwhelmingly strange; although Hopkins is often loosely referred to as a proto-modern poet, his stylistic habits have never been fully assimilated, unlike those of the Modernist mainstream, which derive, ultimately, from French Symbolism and which are now familiar enough to readers of Pound and Eliot and Stevens. Even Hopkins's insistence that the poem becomes more intelligible when read aloud, though basically sound, is true only in a partial, frustrating way; for the poem is extremely difficult to read aloud, requiring virtuoso performance to be effective. (Just such a performance was provided by Paul Scofield on BBC Radio 3 for the hundredth anniversary of the poem in December 1975.)

Yet "The Wreck of the *Deutschland*" is not wholly inaccessible. With patience and renewed readings, it becomes less dragonish; it reveals, in time, the pied or duplex quality so characteristic of Hopkins, offering familiar elements as well as remote ones, simplicity as well as complexity. However elaborate the local detail, the poem's two-fold structure is easily apprehended; nearly all Hopkins's later poems show a similar duality, though usually on the much smaller scale afforded by the division between the octet and sestet of a Petrarchan sonnet. The personal encounter with Christ evoked in Part One is both parallelled by and contrasted with the figure of the tall German nun calling, *in extremis*, on Christ, in Part Two. In stanza 24 Hopkins juxtaposes himself and the nun, the two *foci* of the poem:

> Away in the loveable west,
> On a pastoral forehead of Wales,
> I was under a roof here, I was at rest,
> And they the prey of the gales;
> She to the black-about air, to the breaker, the thickly
> Falling flakes, to the throng that catches and quails
> Was calling 'O Christ, Christ, come quickly':
> The cross to her she calls Christ to her, christens her wild-worst Best.

The poem is a network of contrasts-in-likeness. Hopkins everywhere finds what Scholastic philosophy would have described as analogical relations, demonstrating at the same time what modern psychology would regard as his capacity for lateral thinking. Thus, in stanza 20, "*Deutschland*," the name of the doomed vessel as well as of the nation that launched the Reformation and expelled the five Franciscan nuns, is called "double a desperate name!" Hopkins sees a particular significance in the fact that both St. Gertrude and Martin Luther (in those pre-ecumenical days regarded by Catholics as a wholly malign figure) came from the town of Eisleben in Thuringia:

> But Gertrude, lily, and Luther, are two of a town,
> Christ's lily and beast of the waste wood. . . .

In stanza 30 Hopkins notes that the *Deutschland* was wrecked on the eve of the feast of the Immaculate Conception of Mary, which is commemorated on 8th December. This doctrine (which has nothing to do with the Virgin Birth, as is sometimes thought, but which states that Mary was conceived without original sin) was one Hopkins was greatly devoted to. It had been energetically preached in the thirteenth century by his teacher and hero, Duns Scotus, whom Hopkins saw as a splendour of Catholic Britain. In the final stanzas the scattered and opposed themes converge in a positive, even triumphant conclusion. The drowned nun is transformed into the type of the virgin-martyr, to whom Hopkins directs a fervent prayer for the return of Christ as King in England, or, in other words, the return of the English people to the Catholic faith.

This analogical state of mind relates Hopkins to the intellectual habits of the Middle Ages and the Counter-Reformation. But it has a more familiar aspect, insofar as it looks forward to the secular, verbal and aesthetic analogies and paradoxes that haunted the Jesuit-educated James Joyce. To say that "The Wreck of the *Deutschland*" is a network of analogies is not, of course, to say anything about its quality as poetry. A poem so described might be no more than a collection of frigid conceits without imaginative life. Some of Hopkins's poems come close to inviting this condemnation, but "The Wreck of the *Deutschland*," for all its faults, is not one of them. The poem is driven by intense personal feeling, and

Hopkins assured Bridges: "what refers to myself in the poem is all strictly and literally true and did all occur; nothing is added for poetical padding" (LB 47). This assurance has led to speculation about the autobiographal genesis of the over-powering spiritual experience described in the opening stanzas: "Thou knowest the walls, altar and hour and night." Such speculation has been quite inconclusive; one of Hopkins's Jesuit commentators, Father Devlin, was certain that the experience in question took place long before, during the Long Retreat which began Hopkins's novitiate at Manresa, while another, Father Peter Milward, has changed his mind about it. Having first suggested that it happened when Hopkins was converted to Catholicism, he now believes that it occurred in the chapel at St. Beuno's when Hopkins heard about the wreck in December 1875.[2]

Although "The Wreck of the *Deutschland*" is a heartfelt personal utterance, it requires, insofar as it is a poem, to be read dramatically, which is not necessarily the same as impersonally. And in its dramatic quality it is rooted in the central traditions of English poetry. As a dramatic transformation of urgent personal experience it recalls earlier poets, such as Donne, whom Hopkins seems never to have read, and Milton, whom he read constantly. Here is the dramatically arresting first stanza:

> Thou mastering me
> God! giver of breath and bread;
> World's strand, sway of the sea;
> Lord of living and dead;
> Thou hast bound bones and veins in me, fastened me flesh,
> And after it almost unmade, what with dread,
> Thy doing: and dost thou touch me afresh?
> Over again I feel thy finger and find thee.

This, as we know from Hopkins's explanation, was not the first part of the poem to be written; originally it began with the

[2] Christopher Devlin, SD 12; Peter Milward, *A Commentary on G. M. Hopkins's "The Wreck of the Deutschland"* (Tokyo: 1968), p. 23; *Landscape and Inscape* (London: 1975), p. 20.

narrative simplicity of stanza 12, "On Saturday sailed from Bremen. . . ." But these opening lines, with their combined energy and elaboration, embody his achieved style. Nothing could be more starkly forceful than the opening words, where the syntax is vehemently compressed. They are immediately followed by a syntactical device that is highly characteristic of Hopkins's mature poetry, and a frequent cause of ambiguity or difficulty: the string of phrases in apposition to "God." "Giver of breath and bread" is magnificently apt, and so is "Lord of living and dead." But the intervening phrase, "World's strand, sway of the sea," makes the reader pause. "Strand" can mean either an element of a string or rope, or the edge of the sea; and "sway" can refer either to the movement of the water, or to its rule and government. An interpretation can be teased out to suit the context, but these phrases are not as dramatically appropriate as "giver" or "Lord." Despite the common assumption of twentieth-century poetics that ambiguity is always and everywhere a good thing in poetry, one may question whether this kind of uncertainty, so early in the poem, is desirable. Yet this difficulty is a blemish, no more, in a superb opening. The reader may not fully understand the experience, but Hopkins enacts its significance and intensity.

In the second part of the poem Hopkins applies the Ignatian techniques of meditation to the circumstance of the wreck, vividly evoking for himself and the reader the extremity of the elements and the desperation of the victims. In the words describing the storm in stanza 13 Hopkins is in tune with something very fundamental, even primitive, in English cultural memory, looking far back to the harsh encounters with the sea recorded in Anglo-Saxon poetry:

> And the sea flint-flake, black-backed in the regular blow,
> Sitting Eastnortheast, in cursed quarter, the wind;
>   Wiry and white-fiery and whirlwind-swivellèd snow
> Spins to the widow-making unchilding unfathering deeps.

One picks up, too, the note of a Shakespearean tempest, and the anguished but defiant cry of human insignificance in the face of it. Where Hopkins writes as a dramatic poet, putting into superbly energetic and memorable lines his sense of human action and gesture and pain, then he is strongly and positively traditional. In such lines, where speech and movement and meaning fuse into a single effect, Hopkins is at one with Shakespeare and Donne and Milton among his predecessors, and Yeats and Eliot among his successors. Yet this centrality is everywhere crossed and interfused with idiosyncrasy, and with Hopkins's passion for elaboration. Idiosyncrasy could sometimes produce exquisite effects, as in the final line of stanza 23, which reproduces the elaborate alliterative pattern of the Welsh device known as *cynghanedd:* "To bathe in his fall-gold mercies, to breathe in his all-fire glances." But such local intensities can too easily detract from the total dramatic effect; elsewhere Hopkins's deformation of syntax in the interests of urgency and expressiveness turns into a love of deformation, or pattern, for its own sake. Hopkins's energetic impatience with the English language is often disturbing. As a final example we may consider the closing lines of the poem; we have a set of nouns and phrases in apposition to "King," a few lines back, opening out into a string of words linked by possessives:

> Pride, rose, prince, hero of us, high-priest,
> Our hearts' charity's hearth's fire, our thoughts' chivalry's
> throng's Lord.

This is, in a way, magnificent; but it is hardly English. Hopkins frequently wants to use English with the freedom of an inflected language, and he is here seizing on one of the few vestigial inflected forms remaining in the language—the genitive—and using it in a quite unidiomatic way to enforce a conclusion of extraordinary compression and intensity. In this final line Hopkins also sets up an autonomous pattern, whose effect is more decorative than expressive, based on the alliteration and assonance between the pairs of words, "hearts/hearths," "thoughts/throngs," "charity/chivalry."

Even whilst making these criticisms I have an uneasy sense that they are wide of the mark, that Hopkins, like other major innovatory artists, has established the codes and conventions by which he is to be read and understood, and that it is irrelevant to assess him in terms of his closeness to, or departure from, a supposed Shakespearean norm. This, certainly, has been the defence of commentators on "The Wreck of the *Deutschland*" who have been more concerned to explain and justify the poem than to read it critically. It is not difficult to say that "The Wreck of the *Deutschland*" is, in genre and spirit, unlike any other poem in English, and being in a class of one it cannot be criticised, since criticism, in Eliot's words, depends on comparison and analysis. As a theoretical position in aesthetics, such an assumption may be plausible enough. In practice, though, it seems to me that a poem written more than a hundred years ago which remains partially unassimilable—a different matter from simply being difficult—is likely to remain permanently so. In contrast, the major works of Mallarmé, Valéry and Eliot have been assimilated. Significantly, Hopkins wrote nothing else like this poem. My own, perhaps evasive, judgment is that though "The Wreck of the *Deutschland*" is not, as some enthusiasts have claimed, a great poem, it does contain great poetry. And the reader who has tried to read it attentively, in however imperfect and halting a way, can be consoled by the knowledge that nothing else in Hopkins will present such difficulties.

II

Among so much else "The Wreck of the *Deutschland*" is a formal experiment, an endeavour to work out the "new rhythm" that had long been haunting Hopkins's ear and which he called "sprung rhythm." This is a subject on which it is possible to say a few words or a great many. The essential explanation was set down succinctly by Hopkins in his early letters to Dixon: "sprung rhythm" was a means of preserving a degree of regularity and patterning in verse whilst breaking away from fixed metrical feet:

To speak shortly, it consists in scanning by accents or stressing alone, without any account of the number of syl-

lables, so that a foot may be one strong syllable or it may
be many light and one strong. I do not say the idea is altogether new; there are hints of it in music, in nursery
rhymes and popular jingles, in the poets themselves, and
since then, I have seen it talked about as a thing possible
in critics [LD 14].

Hopkins later summarized his explanation by writing: "This
then is the essence of sprung rhythm: *one stress makes one
foot*, no matter how many or few the syllables." To this summary Hopkins added an explanation of the name: "I shd. add
that the word Sprung which I use for this rhythm means something like *abrupt* and applies by rights only where one stress
follows another running, without syllable between" (LD 23).
"The Wreck of the *Deutschland*" shows the possibilities of
sprung rhythm, and R. K. R. Thornton has drawn attention to
two contrasting instances. In the first, from stanza 31, there
are only five stresses (and therefore five feet) in a line of
twenty-one syllables: "Fìnger of a tènder of, O of a feàthery
dèlicacy, the brèast of the." The effect is light and insub-
stantial, miming the "feathery delicacy." The second example,
from stanza 11, is very different, with six stresses (and therefore six feet) in only nine syllables: "The sòur scỳthe criǹge,
and the blèar shàre còme." This, too, is mimetic, conveying
heaviness and menace; and the juxtaposition of stressed syllables indicates what Hopkins understood by "sprung" or
"abrupt" rhythm in the narrow sense.

In essentials the "new rhythm" was simple and not at all
new, being, as Hopkins acknowledged, a feature of traditional
verse, whether literary or popular. In practice, though, it was
not always easy to see how particular lines should be read, and
Hopkins had to insert diacritical stress marks, a feature that
may have led Father Coleridge to reject "The Wreck of the
Deutschland" for *The Month*. Predictably, Hopkins was led into
more elaborate explanations and defences in letters to his
friends. The effect of these accounts, and the continuation of
them by later commentators, has been to turn something simple
into something ineffable. One has to remember, though, that

Victorian poets and critics and general readers were greatly
preoccupied with metrics and prosody. This was a direct result
of the dominance of classical studies in schools and universities;
the student of Greek and Latin verse had to spend much of his
time on metrical analysis and the resolution of prosodic difficulties, and the practice was readily applied to English poetry.
For some scholars a lifetime was all too short for the pursuit
of metrical questions and, as we have seen, Hopkins intended
the *magnus opus* of his later years to be a study of Greek metres
that would touch upon the most fundamental questions in
aesthetics. One is reminded of George Gissing's novel, *New
Grub Street* (1891), in which the hero, Edwin Reardon, and his
friend, Harold Biffen, both unsuccessful literary men and dedicated classicists, find a special solace in the midst of poverty
in discussing Greek metres. So, when writing to his friends,
and particularly to the impeccable classicist, Bridges, Hopkins
was drawn to make further and further refinements on his
"new rhythm." (He was sufficiently persuasive to induce
Bridges to make his own experiments with "sprung rhythm.")
On such questions Hopkins, for all his originality, was at one
with Victorian literary culture, and on the further side of a
deep gulf that divides that culture from our own. A classical
training tended to make poets far more conscious of metrical
subtlety than of precision of meaning: Swinburne is perhaps
the most extreme example of the preference for sound over
sense. A living poet writing in the English language is likely
to have an acute sense of verbal implication and nuance, but
to be at best casual, at worst quite indifferent, about prosody
and metre. Throughout most of the English-speaking world
at the present time the semantic and syntactic aspects of verse
are highly developed, and the prosodic aspects largely neglected. I suspect that this situation may be at the point of
changing, but that is not a subject to pursue here. One can
remark, though, that Victorian readers would certainly have
denied the name of verse to much recent poetry, however interesting they might have found it as *écriture*. Conversely, the
present-day reader may find things to baffle him in a Hopkins
poem, but is not likely to be much troubled by Hopkins's

metrical innovations; he will probably take the irregularities of "sprung rhythm" for granted and wonder what all the fuss was about. But this was not the climate in which Hopkins wrote.

Metrical analysis continues to fascinate a devoted minority of scholars, and they have found much to preoccupy them in Hopkins. W. H. Gardner, for instance, devotes some eighty pages of the second volume of his study to a minute examination of the "new rhythm" and its possible sources and analogues in many languages. There is a briefer and more incisive discussion in Elisabeth W. Schneider's *The Dragon in the Gate* which I have found particularly illuminating. Professor Schneider shows convincingly that "sprung rhythm" occurs only intermittently in "The Wreck of the *Deutschland*," and that most of the poem is in a fairly regular anapaestic form. Her judicious conclusion on the subject of "sprung rhythm" is worth quoting:

> To sum up then, sprung rhythm, as Hopkins maintained, has over conventional meter the distinct advantages of strongly marked emphasis, naturalness, and flexibility in the placing of accents. Its disadvantages lie in its frequent lack of both rhythmic and rhetorical clarity, which he tried to defeat by means of elaborate markings, and in its lack of subtlety—of rhythmic subtlety from the absence of counterpoint (that is, of any suggested secondary rhythm) and of expressive subtlety from the nondescript status of all except indubitably strong and indubitably weak sounds.[3]

It is certainly true that in many of Hopkins's later poems, particularly the Dublin sonnets, he reverted to conventional metres. Pursuing the discussion, Professor Schneider points out that some of Hopkins's prosodic ideas were extravagantly eccentric. Thus, he proposed that some lines from Bridges's poem, "London Snow," should be scanned in a way that made nonsense of the most natural reading, simply to impose what he regarded as an interesting metrical effect. It is by no means

[3] Elisabeth W. Schneider, *The Dragon in the Gate* (Berkeley and Los Angeles: 1968), p. 72.

true that Hopkins's metrical peculiarities, any more than his syntactical deformations, were always used for poetically expressive ends; he did, at times, show a disconcerting taste for such things for their own sake, for sound over sense. It is no longer sufficient to regard Hopkins as a revolutionary artist whose genius was misunderstood by conservative readers. The situation is more complicated than that; no-one could be more sympathetic to Hopkins than Professor Schneider, but she remarks during her careful examination of his metrical puzzles and contradictions: "one can only conclude that he was wilfully attempting to make the language into a vehicle that it was not."[4]

If Hopkins was an innovator in prosody (though not always to happy effect), he was similarly so in the other principal aspects of poetic and linguistic structure: semantics and syntax. Writing to Bridges in 1879, he expressed his dislike of inversions and of conventional poeticisms such as "ere" and "o'er" and "wellnigh"; his ideas about the language of poetry seem sensible and in line with later critical opinion:

> For it seems to me that the poetical language of an age shd. be the current language heightened, to any degree heightened and unlike itself, but not (I mean normally: passing freaks and graces are another thing) an obsolete one. This is Shakespeare's and Milton's practice and the want of it will be fatal to Tennyson's Idylls and plays, to Swinburne, and perhaps to Morris [LB 89].

Nine years later he still insists: "to write in an obsolete style is affectation" (LB 284). Hopkins was indeed more selective about poetic diction than many of his contemporaries; he does avoid poetic archaisms and well-worn conventional idioms. At the same time, having been preoccupied with words since his student days, and even engaged in a minor way in lexicography, he is ready to enlarge his own diction with words that, if not necessarily obsolete, are certainly unfamiliar. Thus, in "The Wreck of the *Deutschland*" he introduces the Welsh "voel"

---

[4] *Ibid.*, p. 91.

(for a hillside) and the onomatopoeic English dialect form "slog-gering" (meaning "dealing heavy blows"). In his celebrated sonnet, "The Windhover," Hopkins uses such anglicized French words as "dauphin" and "chevalier," the archaic word "sil-lion" (of clearly French origin) for "furrow," and also, if one interpretation of the poem is correct, the unusual contraction "plough" for "plough-land." And there are many other in-stances of the breadth and unfamiliarity of Hopkins's diction. Still, however much Hopkins went to Celtic or Latinate sources for particular words, he kept generally close to the Teutonic core of English; to what he called, in praise of Dryden, "the naked thew and sinew of the English language" (LB 267–68). In his feeling for English, and his capacity for finding old words with a modern potentiality, Hopkins was expressing his pro-found English patriotism and sense of identity. He was also writing and thinking in the spirit of the lexicographical enter-prises of the middle of the nineteenth century, whose greatest monument was the *New English Dictionary*, of which the first volume appeared some five years before Hopkins's death. He had a certain affinity with the ideological proponents of a pure, wholly Teutonic mode of English, like William Barnes and Charles Doughty, though he remained sceptical about their extreme claims. Whatever his occasional theories, in practice Hopkins did what English poets have usually done, which is to play off the Teutonic elements of the language against the Latinate.

Hopkins also knew, by poetic instinct, what the new lexi-cographers had discovered scientifically: that words do not have one or more sharply defined and differentiated meanings, even though dictionaries, for the convenience of their readers, preserve the convention that they do. Although a word is limited by all the things it does not and cannot mean, its meanings are always growing and developing—and sometimes dying—in an organic way. Hopkins was well aware of this semantic fluidity and flexibility, and used it to rich effect in his poetry. This is one reason why modern criticism, based in part on an explicit poetics of ambiguity, has found Hopkins so congenial a subject. Semantic fluidity is, I believe, more effective when meaning runs into adjacent areas than when it forces the reader to try to embrace opposites; as happens, in a minor way, in the second line of "The Wreck of the *Deutschland*," "World's strand, sway of the sea," and much more seriously in the notorious crux, "buckle," in "The Windhover."

It is one thing to treat semantics as fluid, and quite another to regard syntax in the same way, particularly when writing in a language so dependent on a fixed word order as English. Here we encounter one of the most interesting and contentious features of Hopkins's poetic practice, which I have already mentioned in passing. In the preface to his edition Bridges drew rather pained attention to one of Hopkins's grammatical peculiarities as a possible source of obscurity: the frequent elision, in the interests of compression and immediacy, of relative pronouns. Thus, the phrase "O Hero savest!" means "O Hero that savest!" and the line "Squander the hell-rook ranks sally to molest him" means "Scatter the ranks that sally to molest him." As Bridges remarks, in such lines grammar has to be determined by meaning, rather than the other way round, otherwise one could equally well read "sally" as an imperative verb or a substantive. These objections by Bridges have often been derided as trivial pedantry, but I think they are worth taking seriously; they do, at least, make an important point about Hopkins's poetic practice. Later critics of Hopkins have acknowledged that he did indeed break syntactical rules, just as he broke the rules of traditional prosody, and have tended to praise this practice as exemplifying originality and boldness and expressive freedom from empty convention. If this position looks less self-evidently right than it once did, it may be because developments in linguistics during the last twenty years have provided a new sense of the importance of rules in language. Rules may be broken, it goes without saying; but if one breaks too many rules, one may not be still writing or speaking the language at all. The old modes of prescriptive grammar are unlikely to reappear; nevertheless, modern grammar is prepared to assert that certain strings of English words are *not* English sentences, if only because competent native speakers of the language cannot accept them as such, while other strings may produce uncertainty and argument.

For the sake of compression and intensity Hopkins was prepared to treat English syntax as if it were extremely fluid and malleable, with results that are quite unlike normal usage, like the strings of possessives at the end of "The Wreck of the *Deutschland*." There is an unsophisticated but shrewd comment on Hopkins's syntactical practice in an early note by Father Clement Barraud, who had been a fellow-student at St. Beuno's, where he had uncomprehendingly heard Hopkins read aloud from "The Wreck of the *Deutschland*":

> The wildest of all his wild freaks is that, with a notably pure Saxon vocabulary, he chooses to cast his sentences and phrases into Latin order, the fanciful order of Latin verse. Thus—"The rolling level underneath him steady air" means "The steady air rolling level underneath him." "In wide the world's weal" stands for "In the wide world's weal," or "In the world's wide weal." It may perhaps be a question whether this highly artificial arrangement is a beautiful feature even in Latin verse. Still there one always has unmistakable inflections as a clue to the meaning, whereas in English one is left foundering in a bog.[5]

The contrast that Father Barraud noted between Saxon vocabulary and Latin syntax, though a little too neat, is one of the many polar oppositions that present themselves to the reader of Hopkins. There is no doubt that he wanted to treat English as if it had the syntactical freedom of an inflected language; as did Milton, whose tendency to Latin word-order in *Paradise Lost* has been the occasion of frequent and usually unfavourable comment. Here, indeed, is an evident link between Hopkins and Milton, for whom his intense devotion has been the occasion of puzzlement and even scandal to critics who believe that Shakespeare and Donne must be set up in opposition to Milton. This aspect of Hopkins's syntactical practice has been

[5] "C.B.," "Recollections of Father Gerard Hopkins," *The Month*, July 1919.

discussed by a modern scholar, Todd K. Bender, with reference to the rhetorical device called "hyperbaton," which refers to the overturning of normal word order. Hopkins would have been familiar with hyperbaton from his classical studies, and Mr. Bender suggests that he was thereby influenced to use it in his English verse, particularly to suggest the incoherent processes of a mind in distress or confusion, as, for instance, in stanza 28 of "The Wreck of the *Deutschland*." Hyperbaton can be effectively used in highly inflected languages, but in English, which is so dependent on word-order for meaning, it tends to produce incoherence. There were, I believe, other inducements for Hopkins to dissolve conventional word-order than the largely mimetic one of reproducing unusual mental states. Mr. Bender gives an example of aesthetic or dramatic rearrangement in a line from "Carrion Comfort": "Not, I'll not, carrion comfort, Despair, not feast on thee." He remarks: "Here *despair* looks like a verb modified by the initial *not* until the final words in the first line reveal that *despair* is a noun." This was the kind of deliberate grammatical ambiguity that so displeased Bridges, he says, but adds that it was a common technical device in Greek choral odes.[6] These usages can be defended on grounds of dramatic or mimetic vividness; nevertheless, they are what an up-to-date grammarian would call difficult to process.

There is a further discussion of Hopkins's syntax in a remarkably interesting though somewhat inconclusive essay by Giorgio Melchiori, "Two Mannerists: James and Hopkins." The two writers discussed, though different in most conceivable ways, were almost contemporaries and were both somewhat influenced in their formative years by the Aesthetic Movement. The mature style of both James and Hopkins is what Melchiori called "mannerist," relating it to movements in cultural history where:

the ideals of serenity and formal balance are broken by a spirit of uncertainty and search: the search makes for re-

[6] Todd K. Bender, *Gerard Manley Hopkins: The Classical Background and Critical Reception of His Work* (Baltimore: 1966), p. 121.

finement both in themes and in expression, for a subtler and subtler penetration of meanings and attention to details rather than to the structure as a whole.[7]

As he says, the styles of both James and Hopkins were "artificial" in tending to complication and subtlety, almost to the limits of intelligibility, whilst at the same time using colloquialisms, familiar contractions and a conversational tone. Both writers insisted that their writing had to be read aloud to be fully apprehended, and both composed orally; Hopkins in a peripatetic way, James in dictating to a secretary. And at the same time, both devoted their stylistic resources to a specific aesthetic end: the "inscape" of Hopkins and the carefully composed scenic effects of James. In Hopkins's case, at least, one senses a possibly insoluble paradox. In one aspect, his style is a product of speech, and its seeming oddity reflects the difficulty of presenting spoken language in a written form. Speech may be more "natural" than writing, but speech as communication is usually accompanied or emphasised by non-verbal means—intonation, facial expression, gesture, etc.—and can seem incoherent in exact transcript. Hence the immense artifice that writers of would-be realistic dialogue in drama or fiction need to employ to get the right effect of naturalness. With Hopkins, and possibly with James, this artifice may have become an end in itself, and the relation between the "natural" and the "artificial" made more problematical. Hopkins told Bridges that his ideal for poetic language was "the current language heightened"; in his poetry "heightening" produced some startling transformations. F. R. Leavis, freely comparing Hopkins with Shakespeare, wrote that "his strength was that he brought poetry much closer to living speech"; one may tentatively conclude that Hopkins's syntactical deformations may have begun in the attempt to render speech as writing but turned into the opposite: autonomous pattern-making.

A poet may, indeed, do whatever he wishes with language if he gets positive results. It is for this reason that one defends

[7] Geoffrey H. Hartman, ed., *Hopkins: A Collection of Critical Essays* (Englewood Cliffs, N.J.: Twentieth Century Views, 1966), p. 138.

the obscure but richly evocative poetry of, say, *The Winter's Tale*, where lexical fluidity is used for dramatic ends, or the Latinate word-order of *Paradise Lost*. One might even invoke the theory, more familiar in Continental stylistics than in Anglo-American literary criticism, that the very essence of poetic effect lies in stylistic deformation. At the same time, a language is not infinitely malleable; as Elisabeth Schneider has said of some of Hopkins's metrical practices, "he was wilfully attempting to make the language into a vehicle that it was not." If one assumes that a language's identity is bound up in its basic syntactical structures, then it is evident that Hopkins sometimes deliberately imposed a great strain on the English language. There is a relevant observation in a recent study of a major innovatory poet of the twentieth century by a contemporary poet and critic who has himself written a distinguished study of poetic syntax. Donald Davie remarks of the syntactic idiosyncrasies of Ezra Pound's *Cantos*:

> I am far from being unaware of the riskiness—not for the poet only, but for his culture—of playing thus fast and loose with the conventions that govern prosaic or spoken discourse. And everyone must detect the irony in the fact that the poet who came round to writing like this should have started from a conviction that poetry had to incorporate (and surpass) prosaic exactness. Just here, in fact, is a parting of the ways: either we suppose that our grasp on cultural order, as reflected in our language, is too insecure for such departures as this to be tolerated, let alone emulated; or else, we do not. For my part, a decision either way—given that the person deciding has recognized just what is at issue—is equally honourable.[8]

These judicious observations can conclude this phase of my discussion. It is, I believe, no longer possible to assert without qualification, as F. R. Leavis once did, that "the peculiarities of his technique appeal for sanction to the spirit of the lan-

[8] Donald Davie, *Pound* (London: Fontana Modern Masters, 1975), p. 69.

guage." This is a gesture towards Hopkins's Shakespearean qualities. Certainly there is a Shakespearean side to Hopkins, and it has been much discussed by critics; it is apparent in his dramatic directness and sense of the speaking voice; his sensitivity to the meanings and implications of words, taken singly and in combination; his richness of metaphor; and his delicate openness to sensory experience. But there is also a Miltonic side, which is evident in his wilfulness, in his desire to make the forms of verse and language do exactly what he wanted. We can observe it in his metrical innovations and his frequent departures from "the spirit of the language" in matters of syntax. Frequent references in Hopkins's letters show that he loved and admired both Shakespeare and Milton, though he regarded Milton as a more available norm and model, above all in matters of music and metre: "His verse as one reads it seems something necessary and eternal (so to me does Purcell's music)" (LD 13).

Hopkins also invokes Milton in a crucial passage in a letter to Bridges written from Oxford in 1879:

> No doubt my poetry errs on the side of oddness. I hope in time to have a more balanced and Miltonic style. But as air, melody, is what strikes me most of all in music and design in painting, so design, pattern or what I am in the habit of calling "inscape" is what I above all aim at in poetry. Now it is the virtue of design, pattern, or inscape to be distinctive and it is the vice of distinctiveness to become queer [LB 66].

The superb insight of these remarks suggests that Hopkins understood his own poetic practice and its risks rather better than some of his critics. One can add that the Milton Hopkins wanted to resemble may have been the great sonorous musician who so impressed Victorian readers, but that the Milton he really resembled was the bold, assertive innovator in style and diction who fascinated and troubled eighteenth-century critics like Addison and Johnson. "Inscape" as distinctive design or pattern was present in man and nature, where it was evidence of God's designing hand. It was the task of the poet to transform the inscapes of the world into language, to become the inscapes of poetry. Here one may refer to the lecture notes Hopkins made as Professor of Rhetoric at Roehampton in 1873–74:

> Poetry is speech framed for contemplation of the mind by the way of hearing or speech framed to be heard for its own sake and interest even over and above its interest of meaning. Some matter and meaning is essential to it but only as an element necessary to support and employ the shape which is contemplated for its own sake. (Poetry is in fact speech only employed to carry the inscape of speech for the inscape's sake—and therefore the inscape must be dwelt on . . .) [J 289].

In these two quotations one sees clearly the source of the tension between mimesis and pattern in Hopkins's poetry; he loved the world, but he was a poetic formalist. His way of relating the inscape of nature and language has been discussed in an admirable essay by Donald McChesney, who writes, very suggestively:

> Some critics, especially earlier ones, have strained at a gnat to over-praise Hopkins for descriptive power or ono-matopoeic skill. True he possesses both, but his use of language goes far beyond such mere utilitarian functions, and his poetic purposes stretch beyond these into the realm of pure "play," pure pattern, pure energy of spirit.[9]

To this I will add a further remark by another critic, Geoffrey Hartman, who, having noted how Hopkins's poetry is so caught up with the substantiality of things, considered as the traditional divisions of earth, air, fire and water, adds that it seems to be engaged, too, with the materiality of language as a fifth element: "Language, through him, is again part of the body of things, if not its very quintessence."[10]

Forty or fifty years ago Hopkins was thought of as a "mod-

[9] Margaret Bottrall, ed., *Gerard Manley Hopkins: The Poems. A Casebook* (London: 1975), p. 207.
[10] Hartman, *op. cit.*, p. 12.

ern" poet who wrote before his time. His dramatic urgency, his psychological conflicts, his linguistic innovations, his unexpected metaphors, even his dazzling obscurity, all seemed to make him a contemporary of Eliot and the later Yeats and the early Auden. It was a superficial if attractive view which is no longer appropriate. Yet the quotations just given from Hopkins and some of his later critics suggest there is a deeper sense in which Hopkins can be regarded as a proto-modernist. Hopkins was two years younger than Mallarmé, of whom he had probably never heard; Mallarmé believed that poems were made with words, not with ideas, and wrote that "everything in the world exists to end in a book," which recalls Hopkins transforming the inscapes of the world into the inscapes of poetry. Both poets were lonely innovators and explorers of the universe of language. In ultimate matters they were very different, of course; Mallarmé turned poetry into a religion, which Hopkins would have found a blasphemous if not unintelligible notion; among his scattered secular activities Hopkins did not give a particularly high place to writing poetry. But insofar as Hopkins's poetic aims and achievements point towards what Mr. McChesney calls "the realm of pure 'play,' pure pattern, pure energy of spirit," it seems appropriate to invoke, in addition to the Shakespearean and the Miltonic Hopkins, the ghostly presence of a Mallarméan Hopkins.

III

In an undergraduate essay called "The Origin of Our Moral Ideas," probably written for Walter Pater, Hopkins describes all thought as tending towards unity. He develops the idea as it applies to morality, then adds: "In art we strive to realise not only unity, permanence of law, likeness, but also, with it, difference, variety, contrast: it is rhyme we like, not echo, and not unison but harmony" (J 83). It is a remarkably interesting observation because it states in a conceptual way Hopkins's profound sense of pattern, of difference-in-unity, of contrast-in-likeness, which would later be so vividly expressed in his poetry:

Glory be to God for dappled things—
   For skies of couple-colour as a brinded cow;
     For rose-moles all in stipple upon trout that swim;
  Fresh-firecoal chestnut-falls; finches' wings;
    Landscape plotted and pieced—fold, fallow, and plough;
     And áll tfades, their gear and tackle and trim.

All things counter, original, spare, strange;
   Whatever is fickle, freckled (who knows how?)
     With swift, slow; sweet, sour; adazzle, dim;
  He fathers-forth whose beauty is past change:
                  Praise him.

J. Hillis Miller, in his fine discussion of "Pied Beauty," has remarked: "Piedness, like beauty and like rhyme, is a relation between things which are similar without being identical."[11] It is a way of looking and understanding which is fundamental to Hopkins; and whatever roots it has in his own temperament, it also relates to familiar currents of thought. It recalls, for instance, the medieval belief that the world is a divinely created network of analogies. But to come much closer to Hopkins's situation, and our own, one can compare the above quotation from his early essay with one of the most famous and influential critical formulations in the language; the passage in the fourteenth chapter of *Biographia Literaria* in which Coleridge describes Imagination as a power which:

> reveals itself in the balance or reconciliation of opposite or discordant qualities: of sameness, with difference; of the general with the concrete; the idea with the image; the individual with the representative; the sense of novelty and freshness with old and familiar objects; a more than usual state of emotion with more than usual order. . . .

This passage provides a succinct but wide-ranging account of the nature of poetry, both as metaphysical rationale and as explanation of the way in which poems work in practice; most modern criticism in English is implicitly or explicitly indebted

[11] *Ibid.*, p. 99.

to it. By comparing Hopkins with Coleridge we can see that his attitudes were at the same time profoundly personal and part of the mainstream of English poetics. Yet, as always, Hopkins's beliefs were held with his own particular emphasis and flavour.

It will be apparent by now how often in my discussion I have found it necessary to discuss Hopkins in terms of the balance—occasionally the imbalance—of "opposite or discordant qualities." At the same time, opposites unexpectedly come together: as man and poet Hopkins manifests an "either/or" which can become a "both/and." Most of Hopkins's recent critics have been obliged to discuss him in terms of polar oppositions. Thus, Geoffrey Hartman writes that Hopkins "relived at its source the double nature of the poet who is always both popular and learned, natural and artificial, holy and profane"[12]; Elisabeth Schneider divides his best poems between a baroque and a plain style; and Robert Preyer writes of the tension between thought and feeling: "His intellect is keen and his passion for reasoning awesome: one feels that this powerful theoretical bent would have overwhelmed an artist with a sensuous equipment less developed than Hopkins's."[13] In Hopkins's poetry we follow a movement from a sense of diversity contained in a total unity, as in "Pied Beauty," to the later poetry which dramatises the opposition between a soul almost lost in despair and a seemingly absent God, where the bond between them is reduced to dry and anguished assertion.

"The Wreck of the *Deutschland*" might have been a unique achievement; a spectacular outburst, but still fundamentally an occasional poem. Having written it, Hopkins could have rigorously reassumed his self-imposed abstention from writing poetry. It is fortunate that he took the sensible and easier course of assuming that, having written one poem with his superior's approval, he was now free to write others. In his

[12] *Ibid.,* p. 3.
[13] Malcolm Bradbury and David Palmer, eds., *Victorian Poetry* (London: Stratford-upon-Avon Studies, 1972), p. 186.

poetic *annus mirabilis* of 1877 Hopkins began to write sonnets; the sonnet remained his favourite poetic form until his death, and his treatment of it showed a characteristic combination of precision and freedom. Hopkins used the strict Petrarchan form, allowing two rhymes only in the octet, and with a separation between the octet, which presents an experience, and the sestet, which enlarges on it, a duality that was congenial to him. Hopkins clearly found the strictness helpful, and the pattern of rhymes enabled him to compose in his head without immediate access to paper. But he did on occasion, whilst keeping to the rules as he understood them, bend them almost to breaking-point. He described the eleven-line "Pied Beauty" as a "curtal sonnet," while later "sonnets," like "Tom's Garland" and "That Nature is a Heraclitean Fire and of the Comfort of the Resurrection," run to well over fourteen lines by the addition of "codas." Even when Hopkins keeps to the conventional form, as he usually does, the results can be dramatically different from the customary spirit of the English sonnet, as "In Spelt from Sibyl's Leaves," which Hopkins said was "the longest sonnet ever made." Even the sonnets of 1877, with their ecstatic praise of God and joy in nature, are not close to the erotic or meditative spirit of the usual English sonnet. Yet however idiosyncratic his treatment, Hopkins seems to have needed the limits and possibilities of the sonnet form, and when he abandons it he is liable to fall into frigidity and strain, as in "The Loss of the *Eurydice*" or "The Bugler's First Communion." (Though not invariably, as we see in such happy instances as "Binsey Poplars" and "Spring and Fall.")

"Spring" is perhaps the most evidently beautiful of the 1877 sonnets; this poem and "Pied Beauty" provide a good place to begin the reading of Hopkins for those who are daunted by the North Face of "The Wreck of the *Deutschland*." The octet celebrates spring in rhapsodic language and precise Pre-Raphaelite observation. The sestet turns from celebration to a prayer that is almost a vehement injunction; the syntax is complex but quite readable. The central idea is that of innocence, which rapidly moves through several stages. The beauty of spring is like the lost innocence of Eden:

> What is all this juice and all this joy?
> A strain of the earth's sweet being in the beginning
> In Eden garden.

That lost innocence is momentarily reflected in the carefree state of singing thrush and racing lambs. Yet true innocence cannot be attributed to mere creatures; it is better to turn to those, young people in the springtime of life, who are still comparatively innocent in a human way, not yet tainted by the world, even if marked by original sin. The loss of innocence is indicated by Hopkins in a simple but effective metaphor, where the spiritual is precisely equivalent to the physical: innocence, like fruit juice or wine, is sweet in the beginning but can cloy or cloud or sour. (Wordsworth's "Immortality Ode," I believe, lies in the background to this sonnet.) It was a theme to which Hopkins returned in an impressive though unfinished late poem, "On the Portrait of Two Beautiful Young People." The sestet concludes with a sudden shift to the imperative in mid-line, urging Christ to take the innocent young to himself:

> Have, get, before it cloy,
>
> Before it cloud, Christ, lord, and sour with sinning,
> Innocent mind and Mayday in girl and boy,
> Most, O maid's child, thy choice and worthy the winning.

In the urgent commands, "Have, get, before it cloy," Hopkins seems to be reversing the familiar convention of the *carpe diem*, "gather ye rosebuds," directing it towards the preservation rather than the loss of innocence. Barbara Hardy, in a sensitive discussion of Hopkins's sonnets, regrets what she calls the reduction to allegory, dogma or message at the end of "Spring."[14] I would prefer to say that Hopkins drew a conclusion which he regarded as implicit in what went before. The observation and celebration of the octet might have been sufficient for a journal entry but not for a poem; even the almost wholly celebratory "Pied Beauty" ends with a firm

[14] Barbara Hardy, *Forms and Feelings in the Sonnets of Gerard Manley Hopkins* (Hopkins Society, First Annual Lecture, London: 1970), p. 5.

theological injunction: "Praise Him." Hopkins does at least cleanly separate description from conclusion: he does not moralise his observation, like Wordsworth, or eroticize it, like Rossetti.

Even the most selective remarks about the 1877 sonnets cannot ignore "The Windhover," which is probably the most famous, and certainly the most discussed and explicated. It is a magnificent poem, where Hopkins writes with unparallelled assurance and boldness, prosodically, lexically and syntactically. The octet provides a superb mimetic sense of the bird's freedom and mastery on the wing. This much is generally recognized. Nevertheless, the poem has provoked a great deal of argument, not so much concerned with the refinements of interpretation as with establishing the basic sense of the words. This is largely because of the disabling ambiguity at a crucial point in the poem's development: "buckle" at the beginning of the twelfth line. As everyone knows, "buckle" has two senses, and they are opposed and irreconcilable, not mutually enriching. Hopkins, like other poets, enjoyed ambiguities and the multiple associations of words. But he also knew what he wanted to say, and I believe that he did not always realise the confusion he was causing by the insufficiently considered use of a simple noun with several meanings and no clue from the context. I have already referred to "World's strand, sway of the Sea" in the third line of "The Wreck of the *Deutschland*," and there is another example in "God's Grandeur," in the phrase "shining from shook foil." This could refer to a sword used in fencing, or to fine sheet metal, and either might be appropriate. In fact, we know what Hopkins intended because he told Bridges firmly enough: "I mean foil in its sense of leaf or tinsel, and no other word whatever will give the effect I want" (LB 169). Even the most unabashed anti-intentionalist cannot quite ignore such testimony. It is probable that, if asked, Hopkins would have been equally sure which sense of "buckle" he intended, but in the lack of similar evidence speculation has continued. "Buckle" in the sense of "fasten together" gives the sestet, and hence the whole poem, a significantly different meaning from "buckle" in the sense of "give way under pressure." I now refer to the masterly and, I think, conclusive discussion of this crux in Professor Schneider's book. She sweeps aside the idea that both meanings can somehow be accommodated under the banner of "ambiguity":

> To observe that such-and-such a word—*buckle* it is in *The Windhover*—or this line or that image may mean either x or y and to conclude without more ado that it therefore means both is to ignore the requirement of *meaningful* reconciliation, which occurs only if something within the poem transforms x and y together into a z, or when a new enrichment of meaning x is produced by the presence of meaning y. Otherwise one is merely seeing double.[15]

(One might, of course, read the poem in a Structuralist way as an inexhaustibly "open" text, hospitable to all possible meanings, no matter how contradictory; but only at the cost of intellectual frivolity.) Professor Schneider gives very convincing reasons for reading "buckle" as "collapse" or "give way under pressure." In her reading the sense of the sestet is that all the natural qualities associated with the falcon ("Brute beauty and valour and act . . ."), splendid and praiseworthy though they are, must give way ("buckle") in the face of the far lovelier fire that breaks from "my chevalier," Christ our Lord, who is directly addressed in line 11. Professor Schneider also persuades me to read "plough" as "plough-land," the sense in which it is used in "Pied Beauty," which clears up the other troublesome crux of the poem. One then reads the words, "sheer plod makes plough down sillion/ Shine," as referring to the way in which the earth gleams when broken open in the act of ploughing, a phenomenon noticed in Hopkins's journal. In short, humble actions can produce a sudden unexpected beauty, just as dull embers can break open to reveal "gold-vermillion" fire. Such lowly achievements are characteristic of human endeavour, in contrast to the spectacular freedom of the brute creation exemplified by the bird. There is still room for subtleties of interpretation, but I follow Professor Schneider

[15] Schneider, *op. cit.*, p. 147.

in believing that the sestet is a transformation of the experience of the octet, representing a movement from, or through, the physical to the spiritual; or from the natural to the human-and-divine.

The poems written at St. Beuno's provide one of the two peaks of Hopkins's poetic achievement; the other, answering pinnacle, taller and harsher, arose from the troubled years in Dublin from 1885 to 1889. The intervening period, spent in Derbyshire, Oxford, Liverpool, Roehampton and Stonyhurst, formed a flatter landscape, though marked by some notable and finely achieved poems: "Duns Scotus's Oxford," "Felix Randall," "Spring and Fall" and "The Leaden Echo and the Golden Echo" among them. In "Spring and Fall," dedicated "to a young child," Hopkins returns to the theme of transient innocence already expressed in "Spring," with perhaps a stronger hint of Wordworth's "Immortality Ode." It brings together in a single context childhood and mortality, a combination notoriously appealing to Victorian taste, though with no hint of sentimentality. (One may compare Hopkins's abrasive comments on Bridges's "To a Dead Child"; see pages 111–112.) Rather, it addresses the child in adult, measured tones about what later life must inevitably bring, in a way more reminiscent of Andrew Marvell's "To Little T.C. in a Prospect of Flowers" than of most Victorian poems written to children. But in its juxtaposition of the wistful beauty of girlhood and the decaying beauty of autumn, the poem is close in spirit to a masterpiece of Pre-Raphaelite painting, Millais's "Autumn Leaves." There are several references to paintings by Millais in Hopkins's journal, though not to "Autumn Leaves."

Whilst at Oxford in 1870 Hopkins wrote a sonnet called "Andromeda," which, though not of outstanding merit, is interesting enough to deserve mention. It is, for one thing, unique in Hopkins's poetry for using a classical myth, the legend of Perseus and Andromeda; in general Hopkins disliked classical mythology and frequently denounced its triviality in his letters, especially when writing to Bridges, who had a taste for such subjects. He told Bridges that in this poem he had attempted "a more Miltonic plainness and severity" than in his other work. Stylistically the differences are marked; it is written in regular metre, and although the syntax is characteristically fluid, the general effect is of restraint and plainness. Professor Schneider sees in this poem the emergence of the "plain style" that came to final maturity in the Dublin sonnets. She notes "a sharp reduction in the number of descriptive epithets and complete disappearance of the *ad hoc* compound ones that had become one of the hallmarks of Hopkins's verse," together with "a reduction almost to the vanishing point of the parallel, and especially appositional, constructions; only one of these remains, 'her flower, her piece of being.' "[16] Yet despite this new plainness of language, "Andromeda" remains one of the hardest of Hopkins's poems to interpret. "Time's Andromeda" chained to a rock may be, as is usually assumed, the Catholic Church, and the rock may be either England or St. Peter, though the latter is a very odd reading. The rescuing Perseus may be Christ or Gabriel or St. Michael or St. George; the "wilder beast from West than all were" is anyone's guess, though Walt Whitman has more than once been suggested. Obscurity in Hopkins usually comes from his desire to combine and superimpose meanings, or from grammatical indeterminacy; "Andromeda" is, unusually for him, obscure because of its excessively private symbolism.

I believe that Professor Schneider's division of Hopkins's mature style into the baroque and the plain is helpful, provided one realises that the "baroque" style came first, having been born fully developed, as it were, with "The Wreck of the *Deutschland*." It was the natural outlet for Hopkins's energy, his love of elaboration, his dramatic alternations between elation and despondency, his need for palpable tension between aspiring freedom and strict rules. The plain style answered a different need, for direct, forceful, unadorned utterance. He had reason to see such severity as Miltonic, but it was even more Drydenic: "my style tends always more towards Dryden," he hopefully told Bridges in 1887 (LB 267). In no sense did the plain style supersede the baroque; they co-existed to the

[16] *Ibid.*, p. 168.

end, answering different needs in Hopkins's poetic personality, and both were developed to a new and powerful pitch of achievement in Dublin; the former in his confessional sonnets, the latter in "Spelt from Sybil's Leaves" and "That Nature is a Heraclitean Fire and of the Comfort of the Resurrection." The sonnets written as a result of Hopkins's spiritual crisis in 1885 are the point in his development where he touches certain greatness. Though unlike any other poetry in English, they are an example of the kind of poetry written out of personal religious struggle in which the human dimensions of the conflict are so wonderfully evoked that the poems can mean as much to unbelievers as to believers: one thinks of Donne and Herbert and, perhaps, the Eliot of *Ash-Wednesday*. Although these sonnets are intensely and unmistakably personal, they are written with a dramatic power that one can appropriately call Shakespearean. At its most intense pitch, the personal takes on a kind of universality. Eliot, in his essay, "The Three Voices of Poetry," described how at certain moments the first, or personal, voice can be heard breaking through the third, or dramatic voice, as in the last great speech of Macbeth. "Tomorrow and tomorrow and tomorrow. . . ." In these poems I find something like the opposite process, a movement from the subjective to general statement:

> O the mind, mind has mountains; cliffs of fall
> Frightful, sheer, no-man-fathomed. Hold them cheap
> May who ne'er hung there. Nor does long our small
> Durance deal with that steep or deep. Here! creep,
> Wretch, under a comfort serves in a whirlwind: all
> Life death does end and each day dies with sleep.

If there are images of intimate horror, as "We hear our hearts grate on themselves," there is also a hint of reconciliation and consolation in "My own heart let me more have pity on" where, in Elsie Phare's words, "he talks to himself in homely comforting tones, treats himself with something of the charity which he might use towards a penitent."[17] If the dominant

[17] Elsie Elizabeth Phare, *The Poetry of Gerard Manley Hopkins* (Cambridge: 1933), p. 143.

manner is plain, Hopkins still uses with great effect such occasional "baroque" devices as the compound epithet, "no-man-
fathomed"; his syntactical deformations, too, all serve an
expressive, dramatic purpose.[18] The poems are not simple, but
they are not excessively difficult, and there are none of the
riddling ambiguities that trouble the reader of the earlier poems.
Composed initially for and by the speaking voice, they re-echo
in the memory. They are certainly some of the greatest religious poetry in English; but they are also a remarkable expression of a devastating crisis of early middle life, of a desolate
sense of waste and futility and abandonment, where everything
is lost except the courage to endure.

If the confessional sonnets represent a new maturity of the
plain style, "Spelt from Sybil's Leaves," written at about the
same time, is a fresh and astonishing triumph of the baroque.
This, the "longest sonnet ever written," containing fourteen
very long lines, each with eight stresses, shares a mood of
bleakness and near-despair with the "shorter" sonnets. It was
clearly written out of a preoccupation with death and judgment; in the sestet Hopkins evokes his familiar "piedness,"
but now as the occasion of a stark "either/or," not a "both/
and": "black, white; right, wrong"—man must choose between
salvation or damnation. Yet the total effect of the poem is
somehow other; to quote Professor Schneider again: "The
statement of the poem, then, is about choice, but its spirit is not
of choice but of doom."[19] In this poem Hopkins abandons his
familiar two-part structure and, in imaginative terms, unfolds
a single mood, of doom, finality, death. Yet whatever its origins
in actual and painful experience, this poem seems to me a
product of the "Mallarméan" Hopkins; as we read it, the world
seems to melt into language. Semantically, the words are not
empty, nor there just for musical effect; but in their interactions
their meanings fade and they exist as a strange unearthly

[18] With, to my mind, the exception of the final phrase of "To seem the
stranger," "leaves me a lonely began," which remains an inexcusably
perverse construction, despite ingenious attempts to construe it.

[19] Schneider, op. cit., p. 168.

music. The lines become pure poetry in a Symbolist sense, or pure "textuality" in a Structuralist one:

> Earnest, earthless, equal, attuneable, | vaulty, voluminous,
> . . . stupendous
> Evening strains to be tíme's vást, | womb-of-all, home-
> of-all, hearse-of-all night.
> Her fond yellow hornlight wound to the west,| her wild
> hollow hoarlight hung to the height
> Waste; her earliest stars, earlstars, | stárs principal,
> overbend us,
> Fíre-féaturing heaven. For earth | her being has unbound;
> her dapple is at end, as-
> tray or aswarm, all throughther, in throngs; | self ín self
> steepèd and páshed - quíte
> Disremembering, dísmémbering | áll now. Heart, you
> round me right
> With; Óur évening is over us; óur night | whélms, whélms
> ánd will end us.

I am irresistibly reminded of a famous passage from a later text which aims at turning the whole of reality into language, in fulfillment of Mallarmé's aspiration. I mean the haunting evocation of nightfall from the "Anna Livia Plurabelle" section of Joyce's *Finnegans Wake:*

> Can't hear with the waters of. The chittering waters of. Flittering bats, fieldmice bawk talk. Ho! Are you not gone ahome? What Thom Malone? Can't hear with bawk of bats, all thim liffeying waters of. Ho, talk save us! My foos won't moos. I feel as old as yonder elm. A tale told of Shaun or Shem? All Livia's daughter-sons. Dark hawks hear us. Night! Night! My ho head halls. I feel as heavy as yonder stone. Tell me of John or Shaun? Who were Shem and Shaun the living sons or daughters of? Night now! Tell me, tell me, tell me, elm! Night night! Telmetale of stem or stone. Beside the rivering waters of, hitherandthithering waters of. Night!

Hopkins did not think literature important enough to go to the extremes of Mallarmé or Joyce, though he went further along their road than is often realised. But his love of music was more satisfied by actual music than by attempts to turn language into music; we know that in his final years he wanted to be a composer rather than a poet. And, as a rule, he wanted words to mean: the aspect of his nature that might have been fascinated by Mallarmé was balanced by the aspect that admired Dryden.

Though Hopkins wrote few poems, he always developed his craft and scarcely ever repeated or imitated himself; this is one of his great strengths as a poet. Yet in 1887 there was a partial exception to his rule, with "Harry Ploughman" and "Tom's Garland"; Hopkins himself regarded them, with justice, as being excessively contrived. "Harry Ploughman" is a reversion to an earlier and fussier form of the baroque style; it perhaps attempts to do again what Hopkins had done forcefully in "Felix Randall," and to lesser effect. The subject almost disappears in a mass of over-elaborate detail. "Tom's Garland" is still more complicated, and represents the worst side of the baroque, a welter of exploding syntax and frigid conceits. The poem's principal interest is in the long explanation of it that Hopkins wrote, perhaps with tongue in cheek, for the benefit of Bridges and Dixon. But the unsatisfactoriness of these two sonnets merely represented a *reculer pour mieux sauter:* in the last year of his life Hopkins was writing more finely than ever, in both the plain and the baroque styles. The single magnificent example of the latter is "That Nature is a Heraclitean Fire and of the Comfort of the Resurrection," a triumph of justifiable complexity, in both language and argument, in contrast to the elaborate triviality of "Tom's Garland." The poem moves on from the point reached in "Spelt from Sybil's Leaves," where the world is sunk in darkness, and reality itself seems dissolved in language, to an overpowering sense of the centrality of the Resurrection in the whole scheme of things. I quote now Donald McChesney's useful summary of the poem's argument:

Nature is an endless and ever-changing movement of light and shadow, air, water and earth. Man himself seems part of this process. No matter how unique a creation he is, he is destined for oblivion like everything else. This sombre train of thought is interrupted by the joyful and saving thought of Christ's Resurrection. Man will not die because through Christ he is assured of immortality.[20]

In this poem the fact of the Resurrection is set against, not just the Heraclitean vision of a world in constant flux, but, by implication, the world-picture of contemporary scientific materialism. Whatever is doctrinal in the poem is wholly transformed into its imaginative action; at the end, the risen Christ becomes part of the play of language:

> In a flash, at a trumpet crash,
> I am all at once what Christ is, since he was what I am, and
> This Jack, joke, poor potsherd, patch, matchwood, immortal diamond,
> Is immortal diamond.

This must, indeed, be a unique poem: Christian and Symbolist at one and the same time.

Between October 1888 and April 1889 Hopkins wrote his last four sonnets. The one in honour of St. Alphonsus Rodriguez was written for an official occasion of the Society of Jesus, though Hopkins had good reasons for finding something congenial in the subject, whose sanctity emerged from a long, obscure and uneventful life. There is a quite different mood in "The shepherd's brow," which Bridges disliked sufficiently to exclude from the canon of the completed poems; but Hopkins made five separate drafts, and presumably regarded it as a finished work and no mere fragment. Donald McChesney has called this sonnet Jacobean in intensity, and reminiscent of Webster. One might even call it Shakespearean, recalling Hamlet's darker moods. "Thou art indeed just, Lord," is in the line of the desolate sonnets of 1885, though it expresses not despair but a sad resignation to dryness and incapacity, in plain, restrained language which is energised by the tones of the speaking voice. In the sestet Hopkins notes the return of spring, though in far less celebrating language than in his sonnet of 1877. There is a Ruskinian precision in the observation of "fretty chervil" (a kind of wild parsley with fringed

---

[20] Donald McChesney, *A Hopkins Commentary* (London: 1968), p. 172.

leaves), and then a strong echo of Milton, from *Paradise Lost*, Book III:

> Thus with the year
> Seasons return, but not to me returns
> Day, or the sweet approach of even or morn.

There follows an allusion to St. Matthew's gospel, a passage which Hopkins has already quoted in a letter to Bridges: "Nothing comes: I am a eunuch—but it is for the kingdom of heaven's sake."

> See, banks and brakes
> Now, leavèd how thick! lacèd they are again
> With fretty chervil, look, and fresh wind shakes
>
> Them; birds build—but not I build; no, but strain,
> Time's eunuch, and not breed one work that wakes.
> Mine, O thou lord of life, send my roots rain.

I find this poem as powerful, though in a more restrained way, as the more obviously dramatic sonnets of a few years earlier. So, too, is the last poem Hopkins wrote, the sonnet "To R.B.," dated 22nd April 1889, and sent to Bridges a few days later, when he was already suffering from his final illness. It is an example of the kind of poem where the poet writes about his lack of inspiration; Yeats's "The Circus Animals' Desertion," is a distinguished later instance. It represents a final acceptance of the "winter world" of middle age, and shows Hopkins's unflinching capacity for self-criticism:

> O then if in my lagging lines you miss
>
> The roll, the rise, the carol, the creation,
> My winter world, that scarcely breathes that bliss
> Now, yields you, with some sighs, our explanation.

The sonnet indicates a new strength and purity in Hopkins's plain style.

At the moment of his death, Hopkins's poetic art had reached a striking maturity, in the dual modes of forceful plainness and controlled, exuberant play. It is possible that Hopkins would have built on this achievement and have gone on to write many more poems of comparable, or even greater, power and brilliance. Yet given his unpredictable, wilful temperament, and the low importance he set on writing poetry, he might equally well have lapsed again into poetic silence. We can at least give thanks for what he did write, and Bridges so carefully preserved. When Hopkins was beginning to be widely read in the early 1930s, F. R. Leavis described him as the greatest poet of the Victorian age.[21] Hopkins might not have liked such praise; he once remarked: "this is a barbarous business of greatest this and supreme that that Swinburne and others practise" (FL 246). That judgment now, in any case, needs to be qualified, by adapting Ben Jonson's remark about Donne: "The greatest poet . . . *for some things*." If Hopkins embarked more consciously and resolutely than Tennyson or Browning upon the solitary encounter with language, "the intolerable wrestle with words and meanings," his knowledge of the world, his range of human interest, was far narrower than theirs. The careful judgment of a more recent critic, W. W. Robson, seems to me to say whatever is necessary on the question of Hopkins's greatness: "All the same, Hopkins was a great poet. What Arnold said of Gray can be said of him: he is the scantest and frailest of our classics, but he is a classic. His work shows the true mark of the great poet: the capacity for constant development."[22] His was a narrow, even constricted triumph; but he was able, in Marlowe's words, to enclose infinite riches in a little room.

[21] Hartman, *op. cit.*, p. 30.
[22] W. W. Robson, *Modern English Literature* (London: 1970), p. 124.

SELECTIVE BIBLIOGRAPHY

1. *Biographical Material*

G. F. Lahey. *Gerard Manley Hopkins*. London, 1930.

C. C. Abbott, ed. *Letters of G. M. Hopkins to Robert Bridges* and *Correspondence of Gerard Manley Hopkins and Richard Watson Dixon*. 2 vols., revised ed. London: 1955. *Further letters of Gerard Manley Hopkins*. 2nd ed. London: 1956.

Christopher Devlin, ed. *The Sermons and Devotional Writings of Gerard Manley Hopkins*. London: 1959.

Humphry House and Graham Storey, eds. *The Journals and Papers of Gerard Manley Hopkins*. 2nd ed. London: 1959.

Alfred Thomas. *Hopkins the Jesuit*. London, 1969.

R. K. R. Thornton, ed. *All My Eyes See: The Visual World of Gerard Manley Hopkins*. Sunderland: Coelfrith Press, 1975. Contains many remarkable reproductions of paintings and photographs illustrating the visual aspects of Hopkins's life and work.

2. *Criticism*

(a) Collections.

The Kenyon Critics. *Gerard Manley Hopkins: A Critical Symposium*. New York: 1945. Includes essays by F. R. Leavis, Robert Lowell and Marshall McLuhan.

Norman Weyand, ed. *Immortal Diamond: Studies in Gerard Manley Hopkins*. London: 1949.

G. H. Hartman, ed. *Hopkins: A Collection of Critical Essays*. Englewood Cliffs, N.J.: Twentieth Century Views, 1966.

Margaret Bottrall, ed. *Gerard Manley Hopkins: Poems. A Casebook*. London: 1975.

The last two collections contain much useful material, including essays by F. R. Leavis, Giorgio Melchiori, J. Hillis Miller, Yvor Winters, and the editor in Hartman's; and by Elisabeth Schneider and Donald McChesney in Bottrall's.

(b) Books.

Elsie E. Phare. *Gerard Manley Hopkins*. Cambridge: 1933. Reprinted New York: 1967. A short, perceptive early study.

W. H. Gardner. *Gerard Manley Hopkins.* 2 vols. London: 1944, 1949. Immensely detailed and informative, though critically naive and over-burdened with irrelevant material.

T. K. Bender. *Gerard Manley Hopkins: The Classical Background and Critical Reception of his Work.* Baltimore: 1966. Interesting on Hopkins's use of classical forms and rhetoric in his poetry.

Norman H. MacKenzie. *Hopkins.* Edinburgh: 1968. A short introductory book in the Writers and Critics series.

Patricia M. Ball. *The Science of Aspects.* London: 1971. Very illuminating comparative study of Coleridge, Ruskin and Hopkins.

Elisabeth W. Schneider. *The Dragon in the Gate.* Berkeley and Los Angeles: 1968. Essays on different aspects of Hopkins's poetry, containing some outstanding criticism.

R. K. R. Thornton. *Gerard Manley Hopkins: The Poems.* London: 1973. A short introduction in the Studies in English Literature series, just, sensitive and well-informed.

(c) *Essays*

In addition to the material reprinted in the collections edited by Hartman and Bottrall, the following essays are worth attention:

Donald Davie. "Hopkins as a Decadent Critic." In *Purity of Diction in English Verse.* London: 1952; 2nd ed. 1967.

Barbara Hardy. *Forms and Feelings in the Sonnets of Gerard Manley Hopkins.* First Annual Lecture, The Hopkins Society. London: 1970.

Robert O. Preyer, " 'The Fine Delight that Fathers Thought': Gerard Manley Hopkins and the Romantic Survival." In Malcolm Bradbury and David Palmer, eds., *Victorian Poetry,* Stratford-upon-Avon Studies. London: 1972.

3. *Commentaries*

Donald McChesney. *A Hopkins Commentary.* London: 1968.

P. L. Mariani. *A Commentary on the Complete Poems of Gerard Manley Hopkins.* Cornell: 1969.

4. *Bibliography*

Tom Dunne. *Gerard Manley Hopkins: A Comprehensive Bibliography.* London: 1976.

Index

Index